I Am

Stephen Shaw

I Am

A Journey to Enlightenment

ISBN: 978-0-9568237-0-0

My first book **I Am** contains spiritual and mystical teachings from enlightened masters that point the way to love, peace, bliss, freedom and spiritual awakening.

My second book **Heart Song** takes you on a mystical adventure into creating your reality and manifesting your dreams, and reveals the secrets to attaining a fulfilled and joyful life.

My third book **Star Child** offers an exciting glimpse into the future on earth. The return of the gods and the advanced mystical teachings. And the ultimate battle of light versus darkness.

My fourth book **They Walk Among Us** is a love story spanning two realities. Explore the mystery of the angels. Discover the secrets of Love Whispering.

My fifth book **Reflections** offers mystical words for guidance, meditation and contemplation. Open the book anywhere and unwrap your daily inspiration.

In Lak'ech Ala K'in!

~ Stephen Shaw

The Journey Begins

I love airports.

I know many people dread hauling heavy luggage, standing in long queues, facing possible delays, the tedious waiting to board, being crammed into an aeroplane seat, and then being subjected to circulating germs and dry air on the flight.

But I love airports. I always feel the thrill of the adventure and the excitement of my impending destination. When I was a little boy I was filled with wonderful anticipation boarding a plane to fly across South Africa to see my mother (I only saw her once a year). Now as an adult I still can't wait to board the plane, whether for a summer beach vacation, a sightseeing tour through Europe or an adventure in an exotic country.

I am pensively sitting in Heathrow airport in London. It's late and I am waiting to board. I am going back to visit my country of birth one last time. It's sad but poignant, as I will be saying goodbye to a beautiful country and a lovely woman. It's an important flight and a bridge across my two worlds. I am happily settled in London now with a thriving therapy practice and I have no interest in ever returning to live in South Africa.

Two years ago I was torn by a number of unsettling questions: I have built a beautiful house near the ocean, I am living with a kind and loving woman, and life is good – so why do I feel so hemmed in? Why does it feel like there is so much more I need to experience and explore? Should I settle for a life that is *good enough* or do I dare risk everything to find my deepest bliss? What exactly am I looking for anyway?

I made one of the hardest and most painful decisions of my life. I left it all behind in search of something greater, better and more fulfilling. I landed in London, England, seeking fresh ideas, new challenges and a different life.

Leaving something good behind is very difficult. Saying goodbye is hard! Why can't these transitions be easy?

They never are, Stephen. Life is like holding a beautiful rose, gorgeous to look at and lovely to smell, but the thorns will make your fingers bleed if you hold on too tightly.

I am startled by the foreign thought popping into my head. I look up and my eyes are instinctively drawn to a figure standing a few yards in front of me. I notice my heart is beating quickly in my chest.

The secret is learning to let go and stay in the moment. If you don't let go of your past, you will not be fully present in the Now. And yes, I am speaking to you inside your mind.

I look around. People are reading newspapers and magazines, wearing tired faces. Some are munching on late croissants and sipping coffee. No one notices anything. No one seems to be hearing anything, apart from the drone of boarding calls overhead. I am bewildered. This can't be happening!

It is happening, Stephen. I can hear your thoughts.

Did I eat something strange? Are we actually talking inside each other's minds? Pull yourself together, Steve. I look at this man, and think: *I don't believe this is real or actually happening ... so try this for size: how many fingers am I holding out behind my back?*

And just a few yards away, he holds up four fingers.

Now I have two choices: engage with this man or run madly to find the airport police. I am trying to slow my breathing and remain calm. I look around; there is safety in numbers. If it's something I have ingested, it will soon wear off.

I don't know who you are and this is scaring me. What do you want?

I suddenly sense an extraordinary calmness flow over me. I feel my shoulders relax and my breathing deepen. A peaceful energy courses through my body, making me feel a little spaced out. I start smiling like a lighthouse on a dark shore. I feel confused and elated at the same time.

Tell you what, Stephen. I will see you in South Africa. On Clifton Fourth Beach in Cape Town. We can chat then. Enjoy your flight.

I am looking at this man: pure white hair cascading over his shoulders, white eyebrows, white moustache, white eyelashes and amazing almond-shaped piercing blue eyes. He looks vital and fit. He has the typical white complexion and ruddy cheeks of the British, but he sure looks different to anyone I have ever seen.

I look at him and manage to think-mumble: *See you then.* And he turns on his heel and strides away into the busy airport. Suddenly we are boarding and I don't know what to think and there is no one with whom I can share this. I secure my seat on the plane and order a little bottle of whisky and some ice. I settle down for an uncomfortable and probably sleepless night.

Cape Town, South Africa

I am staring at the ocean steeling myself for the difficult conversation ahead. I have been away for two years and I don't think she expects me to return to South Africa. There are still feelings of love and my heart aches. My decision is weighted with guilt and I do not want to hurt her. I am going to leave her the mortgage-free house and house contents. There are no children, she is young and she belongs here. She will be fine.

It is always windy on Bloubergstrand. This beach holds a classic view of Table Mountain. In fact Bloubergstrand means 'blue mountain beach'. Up ahead is the Strandloper ('beach walker') restaurant, if you count an open-air barbecue on the beach among your restaurants. I have fond memories of delicious seafood sizzling on the barbecue, fresh salads and good wine, romantic sunsets, candlelight and soft kisses.

On a clear day it is gorgeous here – white beach, turquoise sea, blue mountain. A piece of paradise. But this world seems small and far away from my new life in London.

The house I built is a few hundred yards away. I take a deep breath and begin the long walk.

Two hours later I am back on the beach. It is raining. I can't distinguish between my tears and the rain pouring down my face. The wind is buffeting my body and I wish I had worn something warmer. My heart feels ripped open and my mind is screaming. Oh, these hard, hard choices! I walk for ages along the dark beach, sobs drowned by the raucous weather.

I am sitting on the wet sand, drenched and emotionally spent. The waves across Table Bay are churning under the faint moonlight. An eerie calmness comes over me. The wind becomes a faint noise in the distance and I can sense my heartbeat. My hand stretches out and it does not seem my own and I notice droplets arriving oh-so-slowly and splashing onto this palm.

I suddenly recall the strange encounter in the airport. What was that message about roses? Did he invite me to meet at Clifton Fourth Beach? What a crazy idea. I wonder if he will be there. I don't even have any contact details. But he knew my name and he knew where I was headed. Maybe it's worth the trip. Perhaps something good will come of it.

I stand up and brush the sand from my clothes. The bed-and-breakfast is not far from here and tomorrow is another day. I will go to the strange rendezvous and see what happens. I look around thoughtfully. I used to love this beach and now it's a bit like a graveyard.

* * *

I open one eye and for a moment wonder where I am. I can hear the sound of waves cascading gently onto a beach. The sun is streaming in and that sky is so bright. The South African sky is so much brighter than the English sky – *brilliant* is possibly the best description. I gaze out the window at the ocean glimmering beautifully in the distance. I glance at the clock: it's past nine. Hope I haven't missed breakfast. I brush my fingers through my hair and splash my face.

I bound downstairs and greet the owner. He seems a little brusque with me. Am I late? "Your breakfast is ready," he says "and I'll need you out of here in half an hour as we are doing some repair work today." I agree cheerily and devour the farm-fresh bacon and eggs. A quick cup of tea and I am out the door. In the parking bay is my guilty pleasure: a hired fire-red open-top sports car. The one thing I do miss in London is the gorgeous African sun soaking into my body.

I am driving top-down, absorbing the lush Cape Town scenery. Drifting alongside the Table Bay beaches, through the Cape Town city centre and then hugging the coastline around Lion's Head. It's an incredible view – rugged mountains rising up on the left and stunning beaches below me on the right.

Clifton Beach is made up of four coves and the beaches are called First, Second, Third and Fourth. When the summer south-east wind blows, the Clifton beaches are usually well sheltered. First and Second are quite private and people often sunbathe and swim naked (although the water is pretty cold). Third beach is known as the glamour beach and is usually populated with gorgeous topless women and athletic hunks playing beach tennis.

I am walking down the stairs from the road to Clifton Fourth. This beach is known as the family beach. There is no nudity and the water drops off very gradually from the beach, making it safer for children. The beach is also longer, lending itself to leisurely walks. My feet arrive on familiar territory with a squelchy sound and the fine sand runs between my toes like a timer.

The pristine beach is quite empty and it's lovely to be alone and so close to my much-loved sea. Small seagulls swoop over the water making hungry cries. The early morning breeze is cool and the hairs on my arms are standing on end. I wonder what I am doing here.

Right on time, Stephen. Let's get started ...

I spin around. How did he find me? He looks exactly the same: radiant, fit, healthy, long white hair, almond-shaped piercing blue eyes ... just one obvious difference.

He laughs and for the first time I hear his smooth voice land serenely on my ears: "Did you know that over 80% of the South African population is of black African ancestry? I simply changed my skin colour to blend with the dominant local population."

Yes, this strange man is now black-skinned instead of white with ruddy cheeks. I can't stop myself from laughing. Partly from the shock of seeing him again, partly because my mind is struggling with the idea that he can simply change his skin colour, and partly because he will clearly *never* completely blend in anywhere.

He is smiling broadly and with such openness. What a crazy situation. I realise that I have not greeted him so I extend my hand. "Hi, you can call me Steve." *I am Jay.* He shakes my hand and peaceful sensations stream into my body, leaving me a little light-headed.

"Who are you, Jay, and what's going on? What do you want from me?"

You called me into your reality, Steve. You seek something that you can't explain – it's something you feel, something you have felt your entire life. There is something wrong with your world but you don't know what. This has been driving you and chasing you for as long as you can recall. Do you mind me speaking directly in your mind?

"No, I am getting used to it. It is nice to hear your voice sometimes though."

Aaaallrighty then ... let's find a nice spot and get you on the rollercoaster.

We sit down together; bizarrely, it feels like I am having brunch with an old friend. Is this how the mind adapts? So quickly? Or is it the unusual peace that seems to emanate from him? Whatever it is, I feel calm and relaxed.

Jay points to the sky and I watch dozens of seagulls congregate, forming a huge circle. Soon more of them pour in and the circle becomes thick and dark. I look around and an early morning ice-cream vendor has put down his cooler box and is staring into the sky. He has seen it too. It is not just me.

This is your first lesson and the most important one. Pay close attention. Those seagulls have formed together in a special way. Is there anything in the circle?

"No, it's just sky. The same bright blue sky that is on the outside of the circle. Everything is just sky but those birds have created a circle."

Brilliant, Steve. This is all you ever really need to know. Hold on to this learning, no matter what you experience, no matter what you go through on your journey ahead.

The ice-cream vendor is standing in front of me offering me an ice-cream. Can't he see I am supposed to be gaining some great lesson? "No, thank you," I say politely. He leans forward like an overbearing salesperson and places a hand on my shoulder. His voice is gentle and kind: "Hold on tight, Steve. Jay is showing you a pathway to ultimate freedom and bliss. This path will often challenge and confuse you but it will be worth it in the end."

I am looking up at the vendor, annoyed, confused, incredulous. Who on earth is this person? I am feeling a little out of control, yet there is still that peace running in the background. The vendor just smiles and walks slowly away, leaving no footprints in the sand.

"Jay, what is going on here? Who are you? Who was that?"

Just a former student. Just a little encouragement. Now back to that circle.

I am trying to focus on the circle but my mind is full of questions. I have moved from my normal reality to something far beyond my world. I feel a little anxious.

Jay's eyes are supportive and flowing compassion. *Tell me what you see. Is there anything but the sky and the gulls?*

"No, Jay. There is nothing but the sky and the gulls."

What about the circle that the gulls appear to have formed? Does the circle have an identity or a personality of its own? Does it actually exist on its own, independently of the gulls?

"No, of course not. There is just sky and an illusion of a circle formed by the gulls. As soon as the gulls fly away that circle will be part of the sky again."

Excellent, Steve. This is your most important lesson. Keep hold of it. No matter what anyone tells you or how things may appear, remember: that circle does not really exist. It is all sky, which is obvious when we remove the birds.

Jay waves his hand and the gulls squawk and disband, revealing clear blue African sky.

Now, let's talk about you. Who are you?

It's a big question. I don't know where to start. My mind is still trying to understand the first lesson. The morning is warming now and I sense that glorious feeling of the sun soaking into my being. I take a deep breath of the fresh, invigorating sea air and stare into the soft sand for a while.

"I guess I am many things. I grew up in a South African culture which dictated some of my thoughts and values. My father instilled in me strong ethics of fairness, justice and hard work. School had definite effects on my way of thinking, as did my university education. The media influences me every day of my life as it circulates social beliefs and values through magazines, films, television, radio and newspapers. And I have grown up in a world of capitalism, democracy and free speech. I suppose this has all contributed to 'me' and built who I am."

Interesting. And what about on a spiritual level? And physiological?

"I inherited certain emotional dispositions and talents from my parents. I am male so I am driven by particular hormones. And I have had exposure to religious beliefs and spiritual values like the majority of us."

So who you are is defined by your genetic inheritance, your childhood, your parents, your schooling and your society, as well as the surrounding culture, politics, economics, religion and media. It sounds like you are the result of thousands of imposed programmes.

"What do you mean, Jay?"

Are you the sum total of all these influences? Who would you be if you had grown up in India? Or been born in a female body? Or had different parents? Who exactly is the real you?

I am wondering what I am learning here. I studied psychology at university and I understand the human mind. What is he trying to teach me?

"Babies and young children are dependent for years on the kindness and security of their parents and society. We absolutely need these authority figures for food, water, protection, affection and survival. In exchange, we readily consume all the beliefs, values and ideas that are pushed upon us by these authority figures. This is called socialisation and it shapes every one of us. It's a necessary part of fitting into society."

Oh, I see ... And who are you beyond all these biological constraints and imposed social ideas?

What's with all these deep questions? Where is he going with this? I rub my eyebrow. "I am unique. All these constraints and ideas made me who I am. However, I am an adult now. I am free to make choices and live my life as I choose. I plan my life, chase my dreams and pursue happiness."

Those blue eyes gaze right into me. *You have been alive for over three decades. You are healthy. You have a good education. You have earned well. You have built a house and been in a loving relationship. Are you truly happy? Are you full of joy?*

I suddenly feel naked and transparent on the fine white sand. I stare at my feet uncomfortably. This is one of my deepest secrets, one I seldom ever throw a glance at: "I have never really felt happy."

Jay is quiet for a while. *When were you last happy, Steve?*

I hastily search through my memories; it is hard to recall happy times. "I remember being a young child, running freely in the autumn rain, dancing and singing among the flowers. There were many moments of such playful abandon. Not thinking or being told what to think; rather, times of just being. Then the happiness got slowly pushed out by the thousands of messages telling me what to do, what to think, how to behave, how to fit in, what to achieve, how I should contribute to society and who I should become."

Do you think there is a central thought or feeling behind all these messages?

"I am never good enough, Jay." I sigh deeply. "And I never feel satisfied with myself or anyone or anything for very long."

The central message of your world is You Are Not Enough. Everyone walks around with this message firmly ingrained in their deepest mind. Most people live their lives unconsciously repeating the same mantra over and over: "I Am Not Good Enough. You Are Not Good Enough."

I wonder if this is true. At school we had to be athletic, academic or physically attractive, or we did not fit in. As adults we are measured by our education, earnings, status, title, possessions and attractiveness. We talk about our achievements and vacations as if they dictate our value. Society frowns upon beliefs and ideology that challenge the political establishment. Magazines dictate ideal body shapes, fashions and social behaviours. The media pummels us with the idea that owning a bigger house, a flashier car or the latest gadget will somehow make us happier or feel better.

That sounds like a crazy way to live …

Am I teaching myself? Or is Jay teaching me? All these thoughts that usually loop quietly in the background of my mind are suddenly becoming clearer.

If the central message from authority figures and society is You Are Not Good Enough, then what is the powerful message that naturally follows?

A flash of insight. I know! "You Must Change. You Must Be Fixed."

Brilliant. The lie that You Are Not Good Enough naturally leads to the deception that You Must Change or You Must Be Fixed. These messages are the disease of your society.

"Yes! And so we are driven to do, to achieve, to attain, to acquire, to compare, to judge, to compete, to buy, to consume and to better ourselves. And we absolutely cannot accept ourselves or others just as we are."

And what are the emotional experiences resulting from these deceptive messages?

"The sting of social criticism and the pain of being labelled and judged usually leads to self-criticism, self-judgement, low self-esteem and lack of confidence. It also results in thoughts like 'I dislike myself', 'This aspect of me is unacceptable' or 'I'll never be good enough'. This often culminates in anxiety, depression, comfort eating, excessive use of alcohol or drugs, and other forms of escapism, attention-seeking or antisocial behaviour.

"I think the majority of us are tired of having to perform and continually better ourselves. We are constantly pushed to improve ourselves in business or at work; and we are always trying to be a better partner or lover or parent and trying to be fitter or healthier or more attractive or more socially adept; and the list goes on. I wonder how many people feel that even with great achievements, status or attractiveness others will eventually see through it all and discover the hidden truth: You Are Not Good Enough No Matter What You Do."

You know what's curious? Almost everyone on this planet feels the same way but no one ever mentions it. You all keep the same insecure secret.

The gulls are screeching overhead, frenzied by a delicious discovery. They look hungry and deliriously happy. As for me, I am feeling quite tired from the warm sun and fresh air, and from having such intense thoughts pulled out of my head like spaghetti.

But Jay is already on his feet. *I am going north for a while; there are a few things I need to do. You've done well today. Let all these ideas settle for a while and we'll catch up in Luxor.*

I quickly get to my feet. Luxor? Where is that? That's not in South Africa. "Jay, we've only just met. When will I see you again?"

When you're ready, Steve. I will be waiting in Luxor. Laso lok je ge!

And then, like it's the most natural thing in the world, Jay shimmers brightly and disappears, right in front of me. I am astonished. What have I gotten myself into? The squawking in the sky draws my attention upward and the noisy seagulls have patterned themselves into a huge circle again.

Maybe I do need time to digest everything. I feel in the mood for a cocktail and some fresh seafood at Blues restaurant in Camps Bay, which is just up the road. Blues offers white tablecloths, palm trees and stunning views of the turquoise ocean. Oh, and excellent cuisine.

I spend the afternoon pondering the teachings and mystery of Jay from under a huge umbrella. The sun is bright in the sky and the sea is so beautiful. Only a few more days of this gorgeous weather and then it's time to head home.

Luxor, Egypt

Life is strange. I am back in London and many months have passed since I met Jay. I am having dinner with close friends and one of the couples has just returned from scuba-diving in Sharm El Sheikh, Egypt. They are glowing and rested and avidly describing their fabulous diving vacation.

Jay! How do I deal with that experience? I cannot even share it with close friends. Who would believe such a story? Instead, I make the usual polite dinner-party talk and we ramble on about the weather, current news, music gigs and films we have recently seen, and books we are enjoying.

After dinner I make enquiries about the diving vacation. It sounds like a great place for a holiday. I have always wanted to see the pyramids and hopefully I can combine a bit of sightseeing with some diving. It turns out that Jay (who I surmise can speak every language) had said goodbye to me in ancient Egyptian.

Life drifts along in a familiar routine: clients in my consulting room, swimming a couple of times a week, a bit of walking in the countryside on weekends, dinner with friends, a good novel in the evenings and snatches of television over the occasional take-away. My father lives with his partner in a nearby town and I visit them once or twice a month. Memories of my life in South Africa twinkle in my mind sometimes and I feel sad but I am learning to let go and move forward with my life.

September finally arrives and I am flying into Cairo in my usual exuberant travelling mood. The ancient world of Egypt with all its mysteries and secrets awaits! I am looking forward to some interesting experiences. And who knows, I may meet Jay along the way.

Cairo is very dry and dusty and feels very hot. There are unfinished buildings everywhere and it's strange seeing so many half-built top floors. The tour guide says that it's a way to avoid paying building tax. He talks me through the usual tourist precautions and insists that I should never drink tap water or eat anything prepared in tap water (like salad). I should not even allow ice in my drinks and must use bottled water to brush my teeth. This should be a fun adventure.

South Africa gets hot, especially in the interior of the country. I grew up in Cape Town with its fantastic warm but moderate climate, very similar to California. It is gorgeous for about nine months of the year and then we get some rain. Egypt, however, gets *seriously* hot. So the tour guide ensures that everyone in the group is suitably dressed in protective clothing, sunscreen and sunglasses.

The first stop is the famous Cairo museum, which is full of interesting objects and unusual artefacts. From here we travel to the pyramids of Giza. I have only seen the pyramids in films or books so it's surreal to see them in front of me as we approach: the size of them! It's a crowded and busy place. Tourists dressed in an array of outfits are flocking around the Cheops, Chephren and Mycerinus pyramids; tour guides are delivering their well worn lectures; and armed guards in military garb are gazing at everyone in an authoritative way.

Our small group has obtained permission to enter one of the pyramids and we are walking down a long tunnel no higher than my body height but wide enough for two rows of people. The air seems to get mustier as we descend and it's a little difficult to breathe. There is a moment of concern that it will all come crashing down and trap us inside. We arrive at a serene and unusual chamber. The guide suggests we say a prayer of respect and gratitude. It's probably a good idea so I close my eyes for a moment. I am awed by the experience but half an hour later I am very pleased to see the sun again.

In the afternoon I am impressed by the enormous Great Sphinx, which is a sculpture of a lion's body with a human head located to the northeast of Chephren's Valley Temple. According to the tour guide, Chephren's workers shaped the stone into the lion and gave it their king's face over 4,500 years ago. It must have taken a long time to complete.

Although it is amazing to view the pyramids and the Sphinx, I am covered in sweat and dust, there are no decent toilets en route, and I never feel completely safe, so I am glad to be ensconced in my air-conditioned hotel at the end of the day. There are some days when a shower feels truly wonderful. A fresh change of clothes and I am studying the dinner menu and wondering what is safe to eat. Luxor tomorrow. I hope it will be more pleasant. Perhaps I will meet Jay again.

* * *

It's a relatively small plane and we occasionally lurch in the sky as if a cosmic puppet-master is playing with our lives. There is an announcement, so I look out the window to see Luxor for the first time and suddenly tears start flowing. There is a warm feeling in my heart, a remembrance, something touching me deep inside. I have no idea why I am feeling like this.

Luxor is so green. It is more beautiful and cooler than Cairo. I like it immediately. I am checking into the Sonesta St George hotel which has a grand entrance of polished marble, air-conditioned rooms, a glorious swimming pool with deck chairs and umbrellas, and magnificent views over the Nile.

I drop my case in my room and head to the swimming pool. Although discretion is recommended in Egypt, many of the tourists are in bikinis and skimpy swimwear. The hotel is more relaxed about dress code as their primary income is from tourists. I throw my towel over a deck chair located next to a table and umbrella. Ah, that first dip in the water! The exhilarating coolness surfs over my body and I dive deep to experience the wonderful tranquillity of being surrounded by water.

I glide to the surface and glance toward my waiting umbrella. It looks like some arrogant person has adopted my deck chair and towel. Then he sits up a bit, smiles and waves to me. I squint in the sun. No, it can't be! I smile back. *How does this guy find me?*

I leap out of the water and we greet each other like old friends, exchanging hugs. Jay looks deeply tanned. I beam a big smile at him. "Hey, Jay." He returns a simple *Hey* and I sense his serene energy immediately. I take up the chair next to him and he passes me an ice-cold drink. Jay is quiet, so we sit in silence, just enjoying the sunshine and great views.

So what is it you do, Steve? What is your mission in life? Your reason for existence?

I raise an eyebrow. No warm-up and straight to business then. How on earth do I answer this? I scramble to put some thoughts together. "I have always been driven by the need to guide people toward happier and more effective living. I studied psychology and work as a psychotherapist in London. Hopefully I am making a small contribution to the welfare of the planet." I shrug my shoulders, hoping this does not sound too dramatic.

And how has that gone for you?

"It has been a remarkable and rewarding journey. People are often troubled by uncomfortable thoughts and emotions or facing difficult life challenges. The greatest gift I can give is to truly listen. It is probably 80% listening and 20% advising. Sadly, listening is a forgotten art in our high speed, overworked, pressurised modern world. And our planet has lost its communal elders who would have dispensed valuable wisdom.

"I am also keenly interested to discover which therapies really make a difference to clients. I want to know what creates rapid and lasting change. There are dozens of conventional therapies, ranging from cognitive-behavioural therapy to hypnotherapy to solution-focused therapy, and there are some compelling alternative and complementary therapies too."

How many of your clients are operating from the premise: I Am Not Good Enough?

I am quiet for a time, gazing into the cool water. "I have to separate the serious clinical issues, like bipolar disorder and schizophrenia, from the everyday counselling issues, like stress, anxiety and depression. Clinical issues require the services of a clinical psychologist or psychiatrist. The majority of clients with everyday problems come to see a counselling psychologist, psychotherapist or suitably qualified life coach.

"To be honest, it is quite common for clients to be driven by the unconscious idea of I Am Not Good Enough. The vast majority of clients are seeking knowledge and skills to change their negative thoughts and feelings or to improve a particular area of life. Of course, these are all strongly interlinked."

How does an ordinary person suddenly become good enough?

"In my experience, if a person feels I Am Not Good Enough or feels Some Aspect Of Me Is Not Acceptable, then no amount of anything will ever make them feel good enough. This includes therapy, a new love interest, a financial windfall, a spending spree, a makeover or a promotion at work. These things appear to fill the gap, and often generate positive feelings for weeks, but they do not create permanent change."

Then how do you heal or fix such clients?

I recall the discussion on the beach in South Africa. "I Am Not Good Enough is a lie that leads to the deception of I Must Change or I Must Be Fixed or I Must Improve or I Must Be Healed. The underlying idea that There Is Something Wrong With Me is usually the result of the programming of society, culture and the media. The truth is, I Am Who I Am and You Are Who You Are. And there is nothing to change, fix or heal."

Look at these trees around the pool and over in the distance. Do you think a tree needs therapy? Do you think this tree here looks at that tree there and decides I Am Not Good Enough? That I should be bigger or smaller or greener like the other tree? Every plant, every tree, every water lily and every chrysanthemum just is. It is what it is.

I am looking at the trees and wondering how nature always seems so serene and nurturing. I remember walking through invigorating pine forests in South Africa and ravishing countryside in England and feeling so peaceful and alive.

A white lotus simply exists. It does not look at another flower and compare, desire, label or judge. The lotus does not struggle to grow or change. It is just a lotus soaking up the sun, drawing in the rain, sometimes losing its petals … and every moment of its existence is perfect. It neither looks at former lotuses or thinks about the type of lotus it should become. It just is. Every day of its life, it simply is.

"I guess self-improvement is society's conditioning. We are taught that we have to *be* somebody or *become* somebody. Honestly, I have felt that pressure all my life, starting with my father's guidance and reprimands. I don't think we ever really change; we just adapt to our current environment. Perhaps it is futile trying to change."

You cannot be anything other than who you are. Trees don't stand around comparing heights. Flowers don't compare colours. There is a great power in total acceptance.

I feel such clarity when I am with Jay. But I have a sense that he is teaching me something much deeper than psychology. I can't quite put my finger on it and I suddenly feel annoyed. Being with Jay is like trying to hold water in my hand. He speaks wisely and has an amazing calm presence but I know nothing about him. His eyes are compassionate and gentle, yet I cannot see *him*.

Remember: Should and Is cannot live together.

There is a screeching in the sky and just above us some hawks are circling. I thought they were solitary creatures but twelve of them are furiously forming a large circle. A hint of recognition seems to register on Jay's face. I am feeling light-headed. Maybe it's too much sun.

I would like to visit Karnak Temple tomorrow. See you there in the morning?

I am getting used to the quick entrances and exits. It's like meeting a magician. Jay instantly disappears from his deck chair and no one seems to notice. A waiter stops by my table and delivers a drink that I don't remember ordering. He places a hand on my shoulder. I am too dazed to be startled. He smiles. "It will all start making sense. Keep your heart and mind open. It will be worth it in the end."

* * *

It's a nice crisp morning and my early start means I can enjoy Luxor before the searing heat of the day. My bus is arriving at the Karnak Temple Complex. The pamphlet describes Karnak as a vast conglomeration of ruined temples, chapels, pyramidal towers and other buildings. This will be interesting.

I walk in and am immediately wonderstruck. It's an incredible place with enormous pillars and statues and I am marvelling at the buildings and temples. How on earth was this built?

You are going to swallow a lot of dust like that, Steve. Impressive, isn't it? Imagine it in its day …

"Hey, Jay …"

I am staring at everything. It is splendid and full of grandeur, yet familiar too. I feel Jay's hand on my shoulder and there is a rush of energy. Everything around me becomes still. Noise recedes into the background. I am aware of a hawk flying just to my left and another just to my right. I seem to be moving fast. Everything blurs until I see nothing but hawks and we are wingtip to wingtip in glorious flight. The sun seems stronger and omnipresent. It's all so bright and so fast and I am entering something incredible and powerful and thrilling. Time stands still and then a shock wave of light explodes within me.

We cover flying a little later in the programme, Steve ...

All around me is sky. I am sitting on something hard and dusty. Jay is laughing softly. *Welcome to the great hypostyle hall in the Precinct of Amun Re. I remember building these colossal pillars. It's a great view from up here.*

I grab tightly onto a jutting edge. "What happened? Are you going to get me down from here?"

You know, for a while we had fun on this earth. Those pyramids we built contain so many secrets. Maybe they will be unlocked soon. Do you remember the Easter Island statues?

What is Jay rambling on about? I hope he is not going to disappear on me.

Steve, do you remember your tears when you flew into Luxor? What was that feeling?

"I don't know, Jay. I just felt like I was returning to somewhere familiar."

Jay grabs my hand and instantly we are on the ground. I am relieved and giddy. Am I supposed to be remembering or learning something? Perhaps there is a memory buried deep in a mystical layer of my mind. I don't know the answer and Jay never explains anything. And it seems there is no point asking.

We spend the next few hours exploring the powerful and spectacular Temple complex. There is so much to see and investigate. We come across a troop of monkey statues and, as if we both know a deep secret, we start laughing loudly and rolling about in the dust and I have no idea what is happening but on some obscure level everything makes absolute sense.

The next day we take a balloon ride over the Nile and fly over the Valley of the Kings. Luxor is so green and lush and the views are splendid. It's a perfect sunny day and we are cheerful and chilled out, and near the end of the flight, Jay, in typical fashion, bids me farewell. He looks me in the eyes, says "Tashi Delek!" and then (should I be surprised by anything anymore?) turns into a majestic hawk and flies away into the cobalt sky.

The Kingdom Of Bhutan

A year has gone by and I have had plenty of time to think about Jay and his mysterious words. It is not hard to understand some of his simpler messages. I have come to realise the futility of fighting against who I am and constantly trying to change, upgrade or improve myself. I like his idea about freeing myself from the constraints of socialisation and completely accepting myself as I am.

My attention is drawn to all the advertising that plays on the idea that I Am Not Good Enough. Advertisers claim that some new piece of clothing, make-up, deodorant or electronic device will make me cooler, happier or more acceptable. Even some therapists are guilty of this: 'My system can change you. I can heal your life. Call for an upgrade.' It seems that almost no one is impervious to the deeply ingrained messages of I Must Improve, I Must Change, I Must Be Healed.

I wonder what would happen to our world if each one of us woke up one morning and realised this simple truth: I Am Who I Am. I am perfect just as I am, thank you!

I am noticing an interesting evolution in my therapy practice. I feel different inside and my interactions in the consulting room seem smoother and easier. I am not intentionally changing anything, yet I am seeing profound and lasting changes in my clients. What has happened to me? Is it something to do with Jay?

I have not had a vacation in a year so I schedule the month of September to visit India, Nepal and Tibet. I am going to buy an open ticket and just go where my heart leads. Besides, I don't know where Jay is, so I want to keep my options open. I hope I manage to meet him again. I have still not shared my experiences with anyone. How can I? Who will believe it?

The flight from London to Nepal is very long, leaving me plenty of time to think. I seem to have started an adventure with no clear destination and I am not sure where my life is going. My therapy practice is thriving and I am seeing pleasing results. My relationship with my father is as strained as ever. It feels like I am in a transition phase, walking an unfamiliar path through a thin mist.

I spend a short time in Nepal surviving the manic driving and then make my way to Lumbini, the alleged birthplace of the Buddha, but it does not inspire me. The world heritage site in Lumbini contains a number of enormous Buddhist temples, each one recently built by a different nation. They are ornate and impressive but these modern structures feel lifeless and they may as well be museums.

The tour through Kathmandu exhibits sacred cows lying among flocks of pigeons in little city squares; temples with huge statues of the Buddha; colourful flower markets; and an abundance of hawkers who relentlessly follow me to strongly promote their wares.

I escape to the Chitwan jungle for a few days to get some space. On the last day I join an elephant safari and we wade through the water discovering plenty of rhinos and other wildlife. I am feeling somewhat disappointed with the entire trip when the elephant driver turns and speaks in perfect English: "What you seek is in the Kingdom of Bhutan." The driver looks remarkably like the ice-cream vendor in South Africa. I return a smile.

My next stop is Tibet but it turns out that the borders are closed for some reason. The woman at the airport travel counter suggests that I visit the Kingdom of Bhutan. She pulls out her map and points out a tiny country cradled in the folds of the Himalayas, bordered by India to the south and China to the north. She mentions that the high price of tourist visas, the limited amount of tourists allowed in the country and the requirement to travel on a guided tour make entry into Bhutan a little difficult.

She also tells me about the concept of Gross National Happiness (GNH) invented in 1972 by Bhutan's former king Jigme Singye Wangchuck. The concept was developed in an attempt to measure the country's quality of life in more holistic terms than the pure economics-based Gross Domestic Product (GDP). The king used the phrase to indicate his commitment to building an economy that would serve Bhutan's unique culture and Buddhist spiritual values.

I am naturally more interested now, and she miraculously manages to secure a tour guide, tourist visa and flight for the next day. The only airport in Bhutan with the facilities to handle international flights is Paro, which is about fifteen miles away from the capital city, Thimpu. I am flying in on the national airline, Druk Air.

The next day I step off the plane into lovely sunny weather and my Bhutan adventure begins. Paro international airport is in a valley surrounded on all sides by steep and beautiful woodland. The airport building is not your typical bleak grey structure but a fabulously decorated Bhutanese building. I feel like I have stepped into another world. I love it already!

I am greeted promptly by my eloquent tour guide Rinchen who quickly explains that all Bhutanese citizens are required to observe the national dress code while in public and during daylight hours. Men wear a heavy knee-length robe tied with a belt, called a gho. Women wear colourful blouses and an ankle-length dress, called a kira. Everyday gho and kira are cotton or wool and patterned in simple earth-toned checks and stripes. The men wear stockings to cover the lower part of the legs. The trainers, I surmise, are a Western comfort.

We jump into the car and Rinchen introduces the driver Jay. I burst out laughing. Rinchen looks at me quizzically, then explains that Jay speaks perfect English, Drukpa, Dzongkha, Sharchopkha and Nepali. Okey dokey then.

Rinchen has a sound knowledge of his country and over the next few days he deftly guides me through the joys of Thimpu. The capital of Bhutan is green and beautiful and the buildings blend charmingly into the verdant environment. Everything is clean and pristine; there is not even litter in the streets. Almost everyone is a Buddhist – either a practising monk or at least living the spiritual values. Even the driving feels safe and gentle.

We visit the thangka art centre, the stunning government buildings, and a number of monasteries where maroon-clothed monks play musical instruments and chant the day away. I notice Jay is quietly smiling. After a few days, Rinchen says goodbye to Jay and me; we exchange hugs and then he is away to meet a tour group at Paro airport.

Jay and I return to the car and we start the long journey to Bumthang. The high pass is a great place to stop and survey the spectacular views. I am feeling happy and relaxed. I notice some birds darting in the sky. "They are black kites," says Jay, following my eye-line.

What is it with Jay and birds, I wonder. As if reading my mind, I hear: *What are we here to learn, Steve?*

I think back to that huge circle in the sky. My supposed most important lesson. Truthfully, I never really got it. "Is the sky representing mind or consciousness, Jay?" I feel unnerved for a moment. Where did that come from?

Bingo! I didn't know Jay could shout in my mind. I feel like I have just passed a test. *And the birds?*

"Thoughts? Feelings? Emotions?" I venture.

And that took you a year to work out? Jay is smiling, a teasing glimmer in his eye. He is quiet for a while, and then: *Bhutan is probably the perfect place to truly understand meditation.*

I roll my eyes. Seriously? What has meditation got to do with anything? I prefer pragmatic techniques to solve problems, improve relationships and increase happiness, not some outdated and antiquated ideas from a bygone era.

Meditation is a path that can lead to bliss and peace way beyond your current understanding. This will automatically affect your relationships, your work, your society and your world in profound and magnificent ways.

I sigh and acquiesce. "Okay, does this involve uncomfortable postures or mantras?"

Meditation is often misunderstood. It is something you do anytime, anywhere. It has nothing to do with whether you are sitting or standing, or whether your eyes are open or closed. It also has nothing to do with religion or other spiritual practices. It is a pure, free practice that is not aligned with any ideology or belief system.

"Well, that sounds more interesting."

Meditation is simply watching the birds.

"Ah, the usual cryptic teaching then ..."

It is very simple. Everything you believe, all your values, every bit of your socialisation and conditioning, every feeling and emotion – all these are just thoughts flying across the sky of your mind.

"Okay ..."

Society has impressed upon all of you the idea that You Are Not Good Enough. However, this too is just a bird circling across your sky. What do you do with thoughts and feelings you don't like?

"We pretend they are not there. We deny their existence. Or we try to escape the pain through shopping, comfort eating, entertainment, drugs, alcohol and more."

Does that make the birds go away?

"Only for a short while. Well, it seems they are gone, but that's just because we are trying desperately not to look."

And what else do you do with distasteful thoughts, uncomfortable feelings and emotional pain?

"If we can't flight, we fight! So if we cannot escape or drown out uncomfortable thoughts and feelings, we usually decide it's further proof that There Is Something Wrong With Me. So we get angry with ourselves, dislike ourselves, even hate ourselves. Or we decide We Need To Be Fixed or Healed or Changed and we start reading self-help books or seek out a therapist."

And what is the book or therapist supposed to do?

"Make us feel better of course! Change or replace our negative thoughts and uncomfortable feelings. Push away the negative thinking and introduce positive thinking. There are so many therapeutic techniques ..."

So ... you either deny or drown out the existence of the birds ... or you try desperately to shoo them away. Have you ever seen a flock of gulls fighting over scraps of fish? They are not going anywhere!

I have to admit that Jay is right. My personal experience and my time with clients have shown me that all the clever therapy and positive thinking in the world does not permanently change thoughts and emotions. If your heart aches with grief, you can hide from the pain, but who are you fooling? If you have low self-esteem, you may compensate by learning strong body language and confident thoughts, but you don't change deep down. In your quiet moments you simply feel like a fraud.

The truth is that bookshops are lined with every Change Your Thoughts and Heal Me strategy in existence. And every few years someone repackages a particular healing system and sells it as the New Big Thing. So many people have done so many courses, attended so many seminars, read so many books and had years of counselling and other therapy ... yet a few years down the line they are still the same people with the same fears, worries and insecurities. Only with a little less cash in the pocket. People don't really change!

So where are we, Steve?

"Parents, culture and the media socialise us so we can fit in and become productive and effective members of society. This certainly has some importance in maintaining our world and avoiding anarchy and chaos. However, we are bombarded and indoctrinated for years with message after message. The primary message that is so deeply entrenched in the majority of us: I Am Not Good Enough. What follows automatically: I Need To Change or I Need To Be Fixed or I Need To Be Healed."

Good ...

"All messages from society are simply thoughts ingrained in the mind. All the thoughts and feelings that result from conditioning seem to be part of us and dictate how we behave and live. If we don't like our thoughts and feelings we do our best to escape from them or change them in some way – the classic fight or flight. Unfortunately this does not work. People simply do not change; they merely adapt to environments and adopt various disguises and personas."

My head is spinning. Where am I going with this?

Meditation is simply watching the birds.

I feel annoyed. Why can't Jay tell it in plain English? Why can't I understand what is he saying? I am trying to grasp his ideas but I feel like a slow student.

Watch the birds, Steve.

It reminds me of my father. He is so demanding and intolerant. He always wants to know what I am achieving in my life; nothing else seems to matter to him. I can never please him, even now. I never feel good enough. Why can't he just approve? Why can't he love me just as I am?

Watch the birds, Steve.

Now I am back in school. I never liked school. Too regimented and stifling for me. The subjects bored me to tears and I made no effort to study. I resented being assessed and graded by some authority figure. What do they know about the real me?

Those are a lot of birds! Jay is smiling now. Is he on the verge of laughter? He better not laugh at me. Jay is laughing now. He touches my shoulder and a light goes on. EVERY ONE OF THESE THOUGHTS AND FEELINGS ARE JUST BIRDS CIRCLING THE SKY OF MY MIND. Instead of denying, escaping or trying to move these birds, my only job is to watch them.

"How utterly bizarre! Is that meditation?" I ask incredulously.

Nothing more, nothing less.

"Are you telling me that my main job is to watch all these thoughts and feelings as they arise in me? Do you know how many I have? Thoughts fly in constantly from the past and ideas stream in regularly about my future. Thoughts bombard me from my interactions with other people and from my own behaviour and from things I see in the newspaper and on television. It is never-ending! And often these thoughts are connected with uncomfortable emotions."

Watch the birds. It is the only way to experience true peace and serenity.

"When and where do I practise this, Jay?"

Anytime, anywhere. You can formally do it with your eyes closed every morning if you prefer. But meditation is best done whenever you remember to watch the birds ... wherever you are. Just notice the birds in your sky. Observe the thoughts and emotions. Watch what happens.

It's a long way to Bhumtang so I am ... uh ... meditating. It's a strange experience as I believed meditation involves mantras and long silences and boredom. It is a wonderful and unusual practice. I often find myself daydreaming and notice my attention is drawn to activities outside the car. But then I remember to watch my thoughts and emotions and I am back being the observer. "Jay, is it alright if my attention drifts sometimes?"

As soon as you notice that you are lost in your thoughts and you bring your attention back to being the witness of your thoughts, then you are meditating again. You are doing it perfectly.

"There are hundreds of thoughts in here. It is like a parrot chattering away constantly. I wonder how I get anything done or find any peace with this incessant noise."

In the beginning there are many thoughts. It's like a waterfall that slowly, slowly becomes a flowing river, then a trickling stream and eventually you notice single droplets.

"Well, if I work longer and harder and really focus, I can get this avalanche down to a light dusting of snow in no time. This is something I can achieve."

Meditation is about Being, not Doing. You cannot chase it. How can you watch harder? There is nothing to do and no goal to achieve. Meditation is just watching, witnessing, noticing. Simply pay attention to your thoughts. Notice when you have become unconscious and then become conscious again. Over time, you will be more and more Aware.

We arrive at the hotel and Jay says he needs to run an errand. It suits me as I am tired from the long trip. I am pleased to sit quietly by the fire and read a good book. Dinner is local fare and rather satisfying. I retire early and lay in bed staring at the wooden ceiling, reflecting upon the day. Sleep enfolds me and in my dreams I am back on the South African beach in the pouring rain, watching a single raindrop land oh-so-slowly on my palm.

* * *

Soft light is streaming through my bedroom window and I peer through the curtains to remind myself where I am. Ah yes, beautiful Bhutan. I feel a bit foggy and am looking forward to a good breakfast.

Jay is already in the dining area looking bright and breezy, tsheringma herbal tea in hand. He is chatting away to the kitchen staff and everyone is having a good laugh. He seems to get on well with everyone he meets. Actually, it seems like he knows everyone.

"Morning Steve!" he bursts out, all smiles. "Big day ahead."

I mumble and smile and reach for my tea. I notice the open English tourist magazine lying near the sunny window so I cosy into a chair and begin reading:

Bhutan translates as 'The Land of Dragons'. The Dragon King (Druk Gyalpo) is the head of state of Bhutan. In English you refer to him as the King of Bhutan. The Bhutanese people call themselves the Drukpa, meaning the 'dragon people'. The current ruler of Bhutan is the 5th Hereditary King, His Majesty Jigme Khesar Namgyel Wangchuck. He wears the Raven Crown which is the official crown worn by the Monarchs of Bhutan. He is the youngest reigning monarch in the world.

An interesting monarch. Do you know that he was educated at the University of Oxford in England? He has some excellent policies aimed at preserving the Bhutanese culture, values and environment. The Bhutanese people are fiercely loyal to their king and country.

I eat breakfast in my usual hurried style and hear Jay speaking aloud for a change: "Just like you watch your thoughts and emotions, try to watch your body and try to notice your environment. Slow down sometimes. Really observe your food. Be aware of how it tastes. Notice how it feels when you swallow. Witness what is happening with your senses. These events may appear to be external but they are ALL BIRDS IN YOUR SKY."

I blink at Jay. It's all birds? Everything is happening in the sky of my mind? That's a bit deep for breakfast.

I try it anyway. I start to really see my food and taste every morsel and swallow and wonder what does it feel like and I notice how my feet are feeling on the floor and my hands on the table and the sounds coming from the kitchen and the noises from outside and I am noticing my thoughts about this and there is so much going on and happening around me and everything seems to slow ... right ... down.

I remember feeling this way on the South African beach and then in Luxor and I am fully allowing everything and being aware of everything and accepting everything ... and there is so much that I am feeling sensing seeing hearing tasting.

I look around in slow motion (or is everyone around me moving in slow motion?) and notice how everything is so quiet, so still, and the colours so bright, so vivid, and there is such a feeling of tranquillity ... it's like I am in another world.

*This is the lesson: The more you notice, the more you witness, the more
you become Aware, and the more fully alive you become. You are, in fact,
entering into Existence itself. It's natural and effortless.*

Jay seems buoyant and animated today. I slowly finish breakfast,
fetch my coat and try to hold on to the magic sensations as we
walk to the car. Wait – it's supposed to be effortless. I surrender
and decide not to hold on to anything or chase anything. Jay looks
proudly at me for a brief moment.

We spend the morning visiting monastery after monastery. It is
amazing to see so many monks in one country. We have lunch
with a wonderful local family in a typical two-storey house with
brightly painted window designs. They regale us with
superstitious tales and glorious folklore which Jay kindly
translates. I am touched by the gentleness of these people. Bhutan
appears to be a wonderful place to live.

Our afternoon visit to a well known monastery is suddenly
interrupted by a military-looking entourage. All the tourists are
instructed to wait outside the monastery and told to stand on the
outer perimeter in a single line. Cameras have to be bagged and
we are forbidden to use them. A murmur rushes through the
crowd. Is it true? It is possible?

We are told that absolutely no autographs may be requested and
no physical contact is allowed. Soon a few ceremoniously dressed
monks appear near the temple entrance. Twenty minutes later the
King of Bhutan arrives and very politely starts chatting to random
and utterly surprised tourists.

The King of Bhutan is standing in front of me. I manage to say
"Hello, Your Majesty." He asks me about my travels and about
the condition of the roads. I find some words and try to appear

calm and sensible. Then he moves further down the line. I can't believe the King of Bhutan has just had a conversation with me. One of the monks, who looks strangely familiar, walks over with a big smile: "The secret to meditation is to watch all the birds. You are doing very well."

Afterwards I start to wonder: Did Jay set this up? Did he know it was going to happen? How much of this is spontaneous? And who is the guy who keeps popping up all over the place? For a moment I feel quite unsettled. My mind is being stretched so far that it will probably never regain its original dimensions.

One step at a time, Steve. I hear Jay's thought softly in my mind.

It's getting late in the day and I am tired of trying to think it all through, tired of trying to make sense of everything. I give up and go back to watching my thoughts and observing the sensory information. And there is a moment – perhaps no more than a few seconds – when I am watching but there is no thought. I am aware but there is nothing. Just me watching. And then it's gone.

"Jay, what just happened? How can I achieve that wonderful space again? How did I get there?"

Do not label your meditation experiences as wonderful or unpleasant or peaceful or agitated. Do not try to grasp these experiences because they will flow through your fingers like water. Only watch and witness and let whatever happens BE. One day this happens, one day that happens. It has nothing to do with concentration or devotion or faith or hard work. Just watch all the birds. Witness. Observe. Be conscious. Be aware. There is nothing to do except playfully watch.

I spend the early evening sitting in the hotel garden, just watching. Everything. All the sounds and sights of nature. My body. My breathing. My thoughts. My feelings. It is something I have never done before; it feels wild and wonderful and very peaceful. I vaguely recall similar moments of wonderment and peace from my childhood. Dinner is a quiet affair and I sleep deeply and dream of a thousand birds in a sparkling midnight sky.

* * *

Our journey back across the country takes us to the awesome and breathtaking monastery at Punakha. It sits alongside a flowing river, surrounded by lush green vegetation and rolling hills. There is a beautiful bridge connecting the monastery to the road side of the river. Jay seems to know everyone and the monks flock around him exchanging greetings like old school friends.

After a while Jay takes me into a place he calls the inner sanctum. Tourists and outsiders are forbidden from secret and sacred areas in many monasteries. There is a group of monks quietly meditating in a stone courtyard, sitting in a very precise diamond-shaped formation. They appear radiant and I sense a serene energy emanating from them. I look closely and notice that each monk is hovering about three inches above the floor. Nothing fazes me anymore. I watch for a while. Jay has got to teach me how to do this.

I hear what must be a group voice in my head, intoning: *It is not about doing, rather about being. When you do, you cannot be. When you be, you can do anything.*

Hmm, guess where Jay got his cryptic style. I cannot make sense of it. It is just wonderful to be in their presence. There is obviously so much to learn.

In perfect harmony: *There is nothing to learn. You are already Here.*

I sigh softly. Most of the time I have no idea what's going on. Yet every day I feel more grounded, calm and peaceful. I look at Jay and he just smiles.

Jay moves to the centre of the monks and starts to glow brightly. A blue light exudes from him and flows over the monks like a celestial river. I am starting to feel strange and a little overwhelmed. This is a world I do not know. A world far from mine. I turn on my heel and escape to a relatively normal garden.

Some time later Jay finds me sitting among the flowers and we chat briefly. Then we bid farewell to the serene monks and settle into quiet driving. I want to ask so many questions but I feel way out of my depth and it feels easier to gaze out the car window. Western Bhutan has stunning scenery, with rice paddies cascading down magnificent mountains and pristine rivers flowing through the towns. Bhutan is one of the most beautiful countries I have ever seen. I watch the birds and savour every moment.

Over the next few days I begin to wonder if we have visited every monastery in Bhutan. It has been an amazing time and we have met many interesting people. Now Jay and I are wandering through the fascinating Paro museum. I receive that familiar thought-energy in my mind: *You need to rest well tonight. Tomorrow we are visiting Tiger's Nest Monastery which is 11,000 feet up in the mountains. You may experience a little altitude sickness.*

In the evening we check into a plush hotel right along the river bank. All night I hear the sound of rushing water and I dream I am carried away in this irresistible flow, at times peaceful, at times uncontrollable, moving me rapidly to an unseen destination.

* * *

In the morning a short trip by car takes us to the base of the mountain. I am expecting a long hike and possibly a climb so I am very pleased to see we have horses. I love riding and it feels good to be in the saddle. Our guide is on horseback and we spend an enjoyable hour navigating the path upwards, taking in the luxuriant greenery around us. Once the horses can go no further, the slow hike begins.

The tea room along the way is a great place for a break and provides awesome views of our destination. Tiger's Nest is a small monastery hung far up on a cliff and overlooking a spectacular valley. It is also one of thirteen small monasteries or tiger's lairs where the Guru Rinpoche (or 'Precious Master' or 'Second Buddha of Bhutan') is said to have meditated.

For the rest of the walk I start to battle with altitude sickness. Perhaps I have a cold too. My lungs are burning and the long descent down the carved stone steps along the gorge to the waterfall takes forever. The pain in my lungs means I am stopping to get my breath every few steps. Tiger's Nest monastery is now above me; it is another difficult climb to the top.

I finally arrive and leave my daypack at the security kiosk. Tiger's Nest comprises many levels of devotion rooms, each with the typical large statues, candles, flowers and ornate decor. I leave my shoes outside and respectfully follow the required protocol.

Although the views outside are stunning, inside it looks pretty much like every other monastery I have seen and I am not particularly impressed. Jay is nowhere to be found.

After a couple of hours I reach the highest level and step inside. The temple is completely empty, which is surprising considering how many people were walking those exhausting steps. There is an elderly monk quietly transcribing into a large book. The decor looks familiar and the dark wooden floor is very clean. I float quietly in my socks. I am looking at the large golden statue and feeling a little bored when I feel a whoosh of energy enter my chest. I stand by the window and tears stream down my cheeks. I am quietly crying and I don't know why. The monk does not seem to notice.

Jay finds me a little later and we take the long and scenic walk back down. We don't talk much and it is really lovely to share time without the need for conversation. I notice that feeling again: there is a subtle change in Jay's energy when he is about to leave. I wish he would stick around for a while and chill out. Jay feels like a good friend to me now and I enjoy his company. Yet I still know nothing about him or his life or where he goes or what he does.

I am off to the Maldives in February for some relaxation and downtime. It's only a few months away and I am hoping you can join me. I have the use of a water bungalow at Sun Island, so you just have to book your flight and get down there.

"That sounds absolutely fabulous, Jay! I will be there." I am smiling. What a thought. Time soaking up the sun, gorgeous beaches and the rolling Indian ocean. Jay gives me a hug, shimmers, and is gone. I am standing at the base of the mountain feeling a bit empty. I stop and watch the emotion for a while. It's another bird, and I am becoming more aware and more conscious. I think I am getting the hang of this.

I see Rinchen at the mountain base with the car. I greet him warmly and we have a quick catch-up chat. He drops me at the hotel and arranges the pick-up time. I need to pack. I have a flight home tomorrow. Back to the routine in London, another cold winter and Christmas with family and friends.

Sun Island, The Maldives

I am in a small yellow-and-blue 16-seater seaplane and we are flying over the beautiful Indian ocean. The pilots are wearing shorts and open-collar shirts. I can see the various deep blue and azure atolls below. The plane is a bit cramped and the air is not the cleanest but we are only thirty minutes from Sun Island. The Maldives! I can't believe I am here.

The plane lands and the passengers and luggage are transferred to a large motorboat. The sea is dark blue and looks deep and scary but as soon as we approach the island the water becomes the most magnificent light blue I have ever seen. The beaches are absolutely white. Palm trees overlay the entire island and it looks like the paradise I envision in my wildest dreams.

I can see the large blue letters 'Sun Island' propped up on solid white pillars. The boat docks and we walk down the long jetty surrounded on both sides by shallow water and then by sparkling white beaches. The reception area is huge and the service is friendly and prompt. I give my name and I am soon escorted to the other side of the island to the water bungalows.

Two rows of water bungalows are suspended on stilts above the water. It's the kind of thing you see on postcards. At the end of each row are two presidential-suite bungalows which are bigger and more plush. Just beyond the presidential-suite bungalows is a restaurant and bar with seating inside and outside and panoramic views over the ocean.

Jay has the use of a presidential-suite bungalow for an entire month. There are two huge bedrooms; a lounge area with long sofas, computer terminals and a television; a little kitchen and bar; and a private sundeck with a hydrotherapy hot tub and a small ladder that accesses the sea below. The sea surrounding the bungalow is very shallow for a long way out so it is safe for swimming, but then it becomes deep dark blue ocean.

There is a lovely cool breeze so I set off to explore. It takes about one hour to walk along the outer edge of the island and many people coast by on hired bicycles. There are tennis courts, squash courts, a gym, a beach volleyball court, table tennis, snooker tables, pool tables, kitesurfing, jet-skiing, bars and restaurants and a few clothing and souvenir shops. I remember now that Sun Island is the biggest tourist island in the Maldives.

I walk back up the main jetty and find the dive centre. The dive centre offers an array of scenic scuba-dives every morning and afternoon and sometimes at night. All the required equipment is available for hire and dive trips are controlled by qualified and friendly Maldivians. Hanging on the wall are descriptions of the various dives along with the weekly timetable. I immediately pen my name to the booking list.

After a delicious lunch, I change into swimwear, grab sun cream and a book and head for the beach. At the front of the island near the approach jetty is a long white beach, plenty of bars and a fresh-water swimming pool. A deck chair and towel are offered upon arrival and I am soon settled in my book.

There are quite a few nationalities on the beach and I hear Russian, French and German being spoken. I am becoming aware that I am probably the only single person on the island. Everywhere I look there are couples in various states of repose; many are holding hands as they walk along the beach; others are playing together in the calm sea. This island is a romantic couple's nirvana.

My mind casts back to South Africa: awesome beaches, fresh air, great food, and a life I shared with a wonderful woman. I feel a bit sad and alone. What is this dream I am chasing? What is it that draws me and makes me so restless?

How is the birdwatching going, Steve?

I scan the beach and there in the distance is Jay, gliding along in his long white robe, hopefully leaving footprints in the sand and not scaring the tourists. His skin is very dark and he cuts a striking figure with his long white hair blowing in the breeze. I wave and shout "Hey, Jay!"

Within moments he is sitting beside me on the beach, and soon I feel that familiar tranquil energy emanating from him. He looks so serene, not saying a word, just gazing out over the ocean. I am reluctant to disturb him.

"There is so much to do here. I explored the island this morning. It's amazing."

Jay is sitting cross-legged on the warm sand, motionless, wordless. I feel the ripple of the cool breeze and hear the gentle swish of palm fronds. The waves lap the shore softly. Half an hour drifts slowly by. I feel a bit agitated. Come on, watch that feeling. Just notice it. Be with it. Watch … the … birds …

"Jay, I think I am going to investigate the kitesurfing. I have been sitting here for a while now and I am tired of reading."

Jay turns and looks at me with those incredible blue eyes. *Today's lesson is about Being. Most people are experts at Doing. Most people are brilliant at being busy. And even when they sit still for a moment they are mentally somewhere else, usually ruminating about the past, planning some future or just daydreaming.*

I feel uncomfortable now. I am not good at sitting still for too long. I am actually pleased that there is so much to do on this island. Jay reaches over and places a hand on my shoulder.

And here comes that familiar experience. Suddenly I am intensely present. I am acutely aware of the sound of the ocean waves lapping the shore the accents of the people chatting around me the soft whoosh of the kitesurfer in the distance the breeze touching my head the feeling of the fine sand beneath my feet the sun on my skin the splash of water from the pool behind me the scent of coconut sun cream the sky so bright before me the slowly moving palm trees ... and in this moment everything feels so serene and intense and full of life.

I have no desire to move or go anywhere. I am filled with a deep satisfaction that I cannot explain. Everything seems to have slowed down. In this moment, this very moment, I am experiencing something so alive, so mysterious, so magical.

Walk with me.

For the first time I know how Jay walks. As I move I am aware of my foot as it lifts, which part of the sand touches it last, how it rises, which part of the sand touches it first, and then the other. How can there be such bliss from walking? It feels like everything moves slowly around me and I find my mind, for once, empty of the constant chatter. I am paying attention to my feet as they walk and noticing my breathing. Breath comes in through my nose, slight pause, breath leaves slowly, quietly.

"Watching, witnessing and noticing are strongly connected to this state of Being!" I squawk gleefully. Something is happening to me. For the first time in my life, I am touching true happiness ... or joy ... or something.

There is nothing but this MOMENT. There is only NOW.

I notice some people looking at Jay. He is standing on the beach at the water's edge and his thoughts seem stronger. I have this tingly feeling and the hairs on my arms are standing up.

Every time you wallow in the past, caught up in should haves, could haves and why didn't I's, you lose your precious connection with Now. Every time you sacrifice this Moment to spend time in your surmised future or fantasies you lose your connection with Life.

People are gathering around Jay. Do they know that he is speaking without speaking? Can they hear him in their minds too?

There is for each of you only this one Precious Moment. When you learn to fully step into the Now, you will discover a peace that surpasses understanding. You will discover that all of Life is contained in this Moment, in the space between your thoughts, in the pause between your breaths.

Jay is looking strange. A Maldivian woman has moved toward him from the circle. She is wearing unusually dark glasses. Perhaps she should not be here but something has emboldened her. "Please help me!" rings out, and now the air feels electric. No one moves.

Jay speaks slowly and kindly to the woman: "I say you are free."

The woman covers her eyes with her hands as if in pain. She throws her glasses to one side, stumbles about a little and then shrieks in her own language. There are tears and smiles and confusing shouts and she runs off as if chased by some invisible phantom.

There is a time for doing and a time for planning, but let not your mind be your master. Your mind is simply a tool to solve problems and work out the best way forward. Use your mind in the Now, and when its job is done, return to this precious Moment. Truly, the whole of Life, and the whole of Existence, is contained in the Now.

Jay does not bat an eyelid. Is he not aware of what just happened? What exactly did happen? I hear shouts further up the beach and people are running toward us. I do not understand the language. Are they angry? What are they screaming?

They are saying I healed her, Steve. They are screaming that I am a god, some are saying I am an infidel. Healing miracles provoke strong emotions. Are you happy to stay?

I shake my head. More and more people are moving this way. People are staring. I feel apprehensive. I do not want to be caught in the middle of a deranged mob.

Jay speaks strongly and with absolute authority: "I SAY YOU ARE FREE!", and it feels like the words reverberate over the entire island. And then without even a glance at me, we both shimmer and are in the water bungalow on the other side of the island.

At once I forget everything. "I just travelled instantly! I shimmered and jumped like you! How do you do that? How did I do that?"

Jay gazes at me thoughtfully. *You are an expression of Life. You are Life itself pulsating in this dimension. I say You are Free!*

And then he is gone. Maybe he is tired or needs some time alone. I stroll down to the Sun Star Thai restaurant at the end of the walkway. I sit outside and order a cocktail. What has happened to the life I knew? Where is it headed? Who could I possibly talk to about this mad and mystical adventure? There is no way back to the life I had before.

I am completely lost in my thoughts when I hear a soft and smooth voice asking "Do you come here often?"

It's an amusing question and I start smiling. Then I dissolve into laughter, which is hardly the best way to meet someone for the first time. It must be the stress of the day releasing. I look over and she is sitting just across and to the right of me.

"I'm Cheryl," she says, extending her hand. I sit upright and try to get some measure of control. "Steve," I say. "I was so lost in my thoughts that I did not see you sitting there."

"Tough day at the office?" I smile again. She is witty and confident. I like her immediately.

"I wish I could tell you. My life has been a little weird and crazy and wonderful lately."

Cheryl is probably about 30, but it's hard to estimate her age. She has lovely shoulder-length brown hair with a slight curl, and the most beautiful brown eyes to match. She is wrapped in a gorgeous chocolate-and-sky-blue sari.

"I am here to watch the sunset and enjoy a cocktail. I am a great listener if you feel like sharing. Have you seen the sunsets here? They are quite extraordinary."

I am probably never going to see this sweet woman again; any minute now her husband or partner will come strolling along and whisk her away to a romantic dinner. What have I got to lose? So for the next half-hour I talk about Jay and the airport and the beach and the trip in Egypt and our tour through Bhutan. I leave out the cryptic teachings. I have no idea what reaction to expect from her.

"You must think I'm crazy. I have not shared these experiences with anyone."

Cheryl shakes her head slowly. "I saw you on the beach earlier. I saw you both disappear in front of all those people."

"Oh," is all I manage to say. I gaze out over the ocean for a while. It feels so still between us, like we are both trying to absorb this story and make sense of it.

We order another cocktail and exchange "So what do you do?" It turns out she is a Music Innovator. She used to be employed by a record company but now works as a consultant to record companies. Cheryl discovers new and innovative musicians and composers and introduces them to music companies. She also works with songwriters and musicians, blending musical genres and producing experimental song mixes. No wonder she is such a great listener.

We chat about our backgrounds and childhoods and soon it feels like I am talking with a really good friend. Whereas my parents are British and I grew up in South Africa, Cheryl has an Italian father and a British mother and grew up in Europe and London. The conversation is easy and flowing and I am thoroughly enjoying her company.

"Would you like to have dinner with me?" She invites me with a smile. "We are right here. If we order soon, we can enjoy dinner while the sun sets."

Wow, we must be the only two single people on Sun Island. I pretend to ponder this idea for a minute, and finally: "I'd love to." I laugh at my own silliness, and she reaches over and slaps my arm.

Cheryl is completely right: the sunset is out of this world. The ocean goes on forever, and it is cosy on the water's edge with the candle flickering, soft music playing and the water lapping just beneath us.

After dinner we walk to the other side of the restaurant with our drinks. It is 9pm and the restaurant always throws food scraps into the water at this time. Small floodlights shine on the green translucent water below. Within minutes dozens of stingrays are flapping slowly beneath us, searching for bits of tasty fare.

We are standing next to each other and I can sense her body and I get that tingly feeling and I am wondering if she senses it too and we are both tipsy from the cocktails and the gorgeous fresh air and it's all a bit intoxicating and I know something could happen ... I could initiate a touch, a kiss, but I like her way too much and I want to be careful and make this something special. I touch her hand: "Cheryl, it's been a long day and a wonderful evening. I really enjoyed sharing the sunset with you. I hope I can see you again."

She laughs gaily: "It was such a pleasure. I need some help tomorrow afternoon at the Araamu Spa. Do you feel like meeting me there at 3pm?" I nod, and without another word she wanders down the long wooden walkway past the water bungalows. She is probably staying in one of the many chalets that hug the beaches.

As for me, I stay awhile, enjoying the fresh sea air and the endless view of the dark ocean. I only have to walk a few yards to get home, and when I do, I will collapse into that huge bed and drift away on the ocean current.

* * *

A new day dawns and the warm sun is percolating through my rested body. I am standing on the private balcony of our large water bungalow watching the to and fro of the waves. Jay finally appears, bearing a large palette of fabulous colours and aromas, and lays the platter of sliced tropical fruits on the table. What a way to start the day!

"Hey, Jay. Where have you been?"

Just helping out here and there. Trying to keep a low profile.

"Yeah, yesterday got a little crazy." I am taking things in my stride now. A miracle here, a disappearing act there, all in a day's work it seems.

It's quite difficult. We used to walk openly on this earth, helping and healing and teaching. The fundamental teachings have always been the same and it takes a while before people awaken and understand that they are free. In the meantime miracles and healings cause no end of trouble.

"What do you mean?"

Everyone complains about some aspect of their lives. Many people pray for a miracle or healing. But when you heal someone, everyone sees only the miracle and loses sight of the teaching. Suddenly there are crowds of people shouting in awe or fear and demanding more miracles. I ask you, what's more important – freedom or healing? Discovering your true nature or having some divine intervention?

"That's easy for you to say. You're like a god or something."

Really, Steve? And you're not?

Wow, what is Jay saying? I guess I'm in the long queue of slow awakeners. Yes, I disappeared yesterday but Jay did that. I am only a therapist.

Is that what you are? A therapist?

Jay is looking across the water at the clear blue sky. I follow his gaze. Oh, not the birds again! There in the distance a circle is forming.

Those small seabirds with the pure white plumage are called White Terns.

"Yep, I see them."

Are those birds or merely expressions of Life?

"I don't know."

Have you ever watched a film, and for a few moments become so immersed in the story that you forgot who you are and where you are?

"Yes, of course."

How did you wake up? How did you return to reality?

"You just become aware that you are watching a story. You return to reality."

What if you are just a story, Steve? Is the label 'therapist' not a story? And being a man? And your appearance? Your beliefs? Your values? What if these are all just stories?

"If these are all just stories, then at some point I will realise I am completely immersed in the film and wake up. I will remember who I am and where I am."

Brilliant! Jay's thought-voice seems to create a powerful ripple in the water and the birds squawk loudly.

And why do you watch all those birds?

Where is he going with this? "Um ... because the birds are my thoughts ... they are my stories. The more I watch and witness all the birds – all my thoughts, emotions, labels, judgements, beliefs and stories – the more I come to realise that they are not me. THE BIRDS ARE THE STORY. And then I can wake up, know who I am and be free."

Yes! Consciousness takes on the disguise of forms until it loses itself in them. And at some point Consciousness awakens.

Jay is clapping, singing and dancing like an inebriated clown on our patio. At once the birds dissipate, leaving clear blue sky.

I feel absolutely elated. Something is happening to me and I am closer to making sense of it. I grab a mouthful of the sweetest, most succulent pawpaw I have ever tasted and the juice runs down my mouth. I jump up and join in the jubilant dancing. Why am I so happy?

We dance around like a pair of delighted monkeys until we fall laughing into the sea. We swim around in the cool water, splashing each other and shouting gleefully at the top of our voices. Then we clamber up the ladder to the deck chairs and enjoy our tropical breakfast, caressed by the warm sun and a smooth ocean breeze. Jay seems to teach the simplest things. Why do I find them so cryptic?

So what are you going to practise today?

I rub my eyebrow thoughtfully for a few moments. "I am going to practise birdwatching today. I am simply going to become more aware of all the birds. Not fight against them, not run away from them, just practise being AWARE. Awareness means being more conscious. Instead of getting hooked into my stories, losing myself and becoming unconscious, I am going to practise AWARENESS today."

Sounds like a challenge. Got some work to do, see you later. Why is Jay smiling like that? For once he walks away instead of shimmering. Maybe it's part of his lower profile.

It's a little later in the morning and I am strolling along the outdoor-activities beach, wondering if I should try my hand at kitesurfing. I join a small queue of people who want to chat to the events operator. It's a bright sunny day with a brisk ocean breeze blowing across the sea.

There is a hustle and bustle and four sturdy Russians bedecked with thick gold jewellery go straight to the front of the queue. One of my buttons is immediately pushed. How dare they? Who do they think they are? Don't they know how to queue? I feel anger building in me. *Awareness, Steve!* I am startled for a moment and look around, but Jay is nowhere to be seen.

What is upsetting you? Their actions or your thoughts about their actions?

"Excuse me, we are waiting in a queue here." They probably won't even understand me. One of the Russians raises his hand and smiles, "I am sorry. We thought you were looking at the event schedule on the wall. It's okay. We move to the back." The Russians clearly meant no harm. They were not being rude. I have only upset myself.

What just happened?

I sigh. One of my stories got activated. It has nothing to do with the Russians. I slid from awareness to unconsciousness and anger resulted. I wanted to practise watching the birds and paying attention to all my stories, and here we are. Awareness equals consciousness, which means paying attention to my beliefs, judgements, labels and stories.

I walk down to the swimming pool. There is one of those interesting bars at the water's edge. All the bar stools are submerged and the counter is above the water. It looks like a spectacular vacation advertisement. It is only eleven-thirty in the morning and people are drinking cocktails. I can't believe it. It is way too early to have a drink! And swimming while inebriated is dangerous and stupid! And there are children nearby. What's wrong with these people?

Enjoying your labels and judgements?

Jay, that's just plain wrong!

It is what it is. All your birds colour your vision and alter your perception of Reality As It Is.

I look around. A couple are gathering their belongings and they leave their cigarette butts in the sand. A German woman is being rude to a Maldivian waiter. An English couple are having a heated political debate with an American couple. Some children are running around screaming and not being supervised by their parents. Don't they know we want some peace and quiet at the pool?

That's a lot of stories. I still cannot see Jay, but he is singing in my head. I don't feel very peaceful anymore.

Why do these Russians wear such heavy and flash gold jewellery? It looks like a mayoral chain of office. Who are they trying to impress?

What is disturbing your peace? Is it really all the differences you see in others? Is it really all their behaviours?

Aaarrgghh! I grab my ears in my hands. Stop it, stop it! What is happening? And it all goes quiet. I hear nothing. Nothing at all. And in this long moment of perfect quietude, I look around and see things as they really are. Humans being. The dance of life. Nothing to do with me at all. My only job is to witness, watch, observe and notice.

Who is creating your reality?

What ...? Are you suggesting that I create the world that I experience? Do I overlay all my own stuff, all my personal stories, onto a world that just is? Is that possible? Is that what we all do? Create chaos out of calmness? Create madness of out nothing?

I sit down on the sand and stare at the gentle waves for a long time. It gets confusing trying to make sense of these cosmic lessons. The birds in my sky. What was that message again? 'Meditation is simply watching the birds. Anywhere, anytime.' Or something like that. It is not about sitting cross-legged in a quiet room, trying to escape the world. It is about *being in the world* with my eyes open, interacting with real situations and events, and mindfully watching all the birds. That's what Jay means about true meditation.

The sun glints off the sea making me narrow my eyes. The whoosh of the ocean seems accentuated and the sand feels soft and warm beneath me. A waiter appears and I order a cold sparkling water with lemon and lots of ice. I still cannot see Jay anywhere.

Jay keeps repeating the same message and it seems my understanding is slowly deepening. He must be a very patient person. Perhaps there are layers in each message and it takes time for me to access each level. Why am I so slow? Why can't I just get it? I laugh softly – I have just judged and criticised myself. Those sneaky birds get in everywhere.

I wonder if patience is an aspect of love? I never hear Jay talk about love. Yet he is very accepting and non-judgemental. Perhaps witnessing and love are connected in some way. I lay back on my towel, put my sunhat over my face and drift away. It will probably all make sense in time.

* * *

It's approaching two in the afternoon and I am having lunch at the delightful restaurant near the swimming pool. Growing up in South Africa taught me to appreciate a good piece of meat and I have a penchant for steak. For me, the taste of South African Karoo lamb and beef biltong (strips of dried meat) are unsurpassed anywhere in the world.

I notice a European couple at another table arguing about the benefits of vegetarianism. Snippets of the intense conversation fly toward me: "… red meat is not good for your health … it's the only moral option for our planet …" I feel my hackles rise. Why do people have to lecture others? Why can't they go outside? I have enjoyed good quality meat all my life and I am in perfect health!

Aha! A slow smile lights up my face. They are trading stories with each other. And my stories started to react ...

All conflict is the result of stories clashing ...

If I am truly aware, truly present, truly conscious, then I can simply notice my stories and notice other people's stories. THEY ARE JUST STORIES. Just birds in the sky. I don't have to pretend my stories don't exist or deny them or push them away. I can just notice and witness all the stories.

All conflict is the result of stories clashing ...

Serenity settles upon me like a soft butterfly. The atmosphere becomes really still and peaceful. I look at the couple, smile and sense an empathic connection with them. They are probably worried about their health. It's *their* story and has nothing to do with me.

I look up and see Jay walking far down the beach, his white hair luminous in the sun. Somehow I know that he is smiling. I hear his whisper: *What is the sound of one hand clapping?* I eat my steak thoughtfully. I guess only Jay knows the answer to that question.

I suddenly recall that I have a date with Cheryl at the spa. It's a short stroll past the tennis courts and I arrive ten minutes early. She is waiting in the reception, beaming and radiant. "Hi," she says, and plants a big kiss firmly on my cheek. I return a kiss. "Hey, Cheryl. It's lovely to see you again."

She seems a little unsure as she asks "How do you feel about learning massage? I have booked us lessons. My treat." What a nice surprise. "I love massages. Sounds like a wonderful idea. Thank you."

We have a brief chat near the water fountain and then we are whisked away to change into bathrobes and slippers. A professionally dressed Thai woman collects us and we are escorted down the stone path. The spa has been tastefully decorated using dark wood, lush green plants and Zen-like fountains and statues, with thatch-roof gazebos behind private walls. It is a world within a world.

We enter our private area. There is a stone bath recessed into the ground and a shower that seems sculpted into a rock pillar and a lily-covered pond on either side of the little walkway. Tall palms sway overhead. Two Thai masseuses smile sweetly, beckoning us to the massage beds.

They are used to nudity – it's their business – and they ask us to disrobe. Uh-oh. I don't know Cheryl that well. Is this one of my socially conditioned judgements? Cheryl throws off her robe and lays on her table. I do the same. I glance across at her. She has a very attractive body. She smiles playfully at me. I let go of my story and I bring my awareness to reality as it is. It is beautiful lying here naked next to such a wonderful person.

We are both enjoying a superb Thai massage on our backs and legs. Half an hour disappears and I wish it would go on forever. This is a savvy way of teaching massage, as we are about to learn the very massage we have just experienced. Cheryl volunteers to go first. I feel the seasoned hands of the masseuse and hear the simple English instructions, and then I feel Cheryl's smooth hands moving over my back.

I try to bring my awareness to this moment. A flurry of thoughts run through my mind. I don't know her. I am naked in front of her and two Thai women. What is she thinking about my body? And this situation? Come on, witness these thoughts. Don't fight them. Notice the emotions. Isn't this all completely natural?

*Steve, witness not just your thoughts and emotions (your inner world)
but also the information coming in through your senses (your outer
world). Otherwise you will be trapped in your chattering mind.* Thanks
Jay, I mentally whisper.

I notice the sound of the wind blowing softly through the trees
and the feel of the table underneath me. I see the pretty painted
toes of one of the women as she kneads my neck. I can smell the
sweet aroma of the massage oil – it is jasmine? honeysuckle? I feel
Cheryl's hands moving slowly over my back now, learning,
increasing in confidence. I am aware of a sensual feeling in my
skin and muscles. My body is deeply relaxed and I feel like a cat
caught in a luscious sunbeam.

Do you see how your stories conflict with What Is?

My thoughts feel a bit dreamy now. "That's really good, Cheryl,"
I mutter. Jay is right. Noticing what is actually happening and
being present with What Is, has caused my stories to subside.
What Is happening now, in this Moment, is exquisite.

I hear the soft voice from some faraway land: "Time to swap
around." Really? Was that 45 minutes? I get up slowly, put a towel
around my waist and move to the other table. Cheryl is lying on
her tummy, absolutely naked and gorgeous. I watch the Thai
instructor for a while, warm some oil in my hands and begin
using my palms to make silky circles along the contour of
Cheryl's back.

I notice how my hands feel on her velvety skin as they travel up
her neck into her hairline and then follow the shoulders and she
quivers faintly as my hands travel down either side of her spine
and I am fully present in this Moment hearing the caws of a bird
somewhere to my right and the babbling of a stream and my own

breathing and the sensual feeling in my hands and arms and I sense every smidgen of her tanned body and it feels like I am moving in slow motion and the garden seems so vivid and green and the air feels alive and a wonderful expansive peacefulness is flowing through me.

Well done, Jay whispers gently. *Now you are getting it. Sometimes there will be no birds. Some people call this No-Mind or the Space Between Thoughts. It often occurs in the Moment when you are fully Present, in the Moment when you are fully conversing with Reality As It Is.*

I hear more massage instruction and then my hands are moving with slow, delicious strokes over Cheryl's thighs and calves, and I notice it is kind of effortless. The more I listen and then place my attention on the stroke, the easier and more flowing it becomes. I open my awareness and watch my hands and the massage seems to be happening by itself. There is nothing to chase or achieve. I am just *being,* and it's liberating and perfect. Cheryl purrs contentedly.

Warm water has been tapped into the stone bath and there are candles burning on the edge with little flowers floating on the surface. The Thai masseuses gesture towards the bath, and Cheryl and I walk like two delighted nature spirits and dip into our lake of pleasure.

We are left alone to luxuriate in the stone bath. I feel so carefree and light-hearted. What a natural way for two people to spend time. No agendas and no stories. Is this the freedom Jay talks about? Half an hour later a pot of jasmine tea arrives and we sup in jungle bliss. When the water cools and our hands are wrinkly, we jump out and shower at the stone pillar and then find our bathrobes.

After we are back in our clothes, we sit for a while in the spacious tea room. Soon warm rolled-up lemon-drenched face cloths arrive, along with another pot of jasmine tea. I grin at Cheryl. "I am definitely coming back here soon." Eventually we lug our refreshed but weary bodies out of the spa.

Cheryl asks if I feel in the mood for a walk. I nod, and we meander along the beach until we arrive at the Sun Star restaurant. "I love the sunsets," she says, smiling at me. I take her hand and we find a table near the water's edge. We enjoy a couple of cocktails and a slow candlelit dinner as the sky transforms into beautiful shades and hues. Sleep will come easy for me tonight.

* * *

I pad out of bed and have a long stretch ... I feel fantastic! I am alone for breakfast and it's a chance to mentally catch up with the whirlwind that has become my life. So much seems to be happening ... first Jay and his mystical teachings ... and now Cheryl. I am learning to flow with life as it presents itself. In the kitchen there is a bright yellow note flapping on the fridge door: *Surrender.* I wonder if the note has just appeared or if Jay placed it here earlier?

I am looking forward to my first Maldivian scuba-dive this morning. I love the ocean, and being underwater is so relaxing and tranquil. I leave the bungalow in good time as the dive centre is on the other side of the island. It is sunny and the sky is clear – a good sign. The sea looks calm and I am hoping the currents are gentle today.

I arrive at the dive centre and it's quite busy. People are standing in a queue for wetsuits, fins, weight belts and buoyancy compensating jackets; instructors are checking air tanks; and assistants are washing down the boat. I have my own mask and snorkel but I hire the rest of the equipment. Soon everyone clambers aboard and we settle down to the lulling rhythm of the journey.

A shoal of dolphins glides past and there is a whirr of cameras. It is tempting to jump overboard but the Maldivians have a strict policy about protecting their marine life and coral reefs. However, about ten minutes later an instructor shouts "whale shark!", which is a rare sighting, and there is a mad scramble to get into the water (no time for tanks). We cruise the surface of the ocean like paparazzi, some of us making deep breath-hold dives. The whale shark is about eight yards down but moves slowly so it is easy to make out the flecked skin.

Half an hour later our formal dive begins, and it's so peaceful and wondrous to descend into the crystal-clear Maldivian water. We tour along the reef and are greeted by a wide array of brightly coloured plants and fish; some are quite bold while others dart just out of reach. We encounter an octopus, a few small sharks and plenty of orange clown fish with their trademark three-white-bars.

We are only fifteen metres under water and the instructor signals us to lie on the ocean floor and keep very still. Soon enormous manta rays are flapping gently above us, exposing their expansive white underbellies. Dozens of these magnificent creatures cruise closely by, seemingly without fear. I am in awe. This is the best dive of my life!

It's a long trip back to the island so I strip off my wetsuit and catch the sun. There are many contented smiles on board; everyone feels tired but happy. Occasionally we are caught by some cool ocean spray, and gradually the deep blue sea changes to an alluring turquoise with white foam. We are back at Sun Island.

Diving generates a healthy appetite, so I rinse my gear, return it, and make my way to the restaurant near the dive centre. The restaurant is surrounded by a wooden walkway and relatively shallow water. Some tourists are completing their diving training and I can see schools of bright fish fluttering around them.

There against the railing, in a lovely white cotton dress covering her purple bikini, is Cheryl, looking as radiant as the sun. "I hope you don't think I am stalking you," she says with a grin. "Hey, Cheryl." I smile. My hair is still wet and dripping as I lean forward and give her a kiss on the cheek.

We find a table with an umbrella, order ice-cold drinks and peruse the menu. After the waiter departs, Cheryl asks me about the dive. I regale her with this morning's marvellous undersea adventure and the beautiful manta rays, and she listens with rapt fascination.

The food arrives and the conversation becomes interesting. I ask Cheryl about her professional life. She works in recording studios in London, New York and Florence. Much of her work is in London where she rents a flat, but she owns an apartment in Florence which she is reluctant to give up. In New York she stays with a close friend in a small penthouse suite. It's a good life which suits her well.

Like most of us, she has had a couple of heartbreaks. She married young, believing it would be for life, but he was unfaithful, which brought up all sorts of questions about love, trust and commitment. I sigh knowingly ... I have been down that road. Cheryl decided to keep the faith, stay true to her values and say goodbye to him. She discovered that life does indeed go on.

I smile. Cheryl's values are music to my ears. I have been around long enough to know that honesty and integrity create the crucial foundation in any relationship. I prefer to build my relationships on solid rock these days, not quicksand. I feel a bit relieved. Cheryl is a trustworthy person and I enjoy her company. Now I know there can be more.

We chat in our usual easy and flowing way, learning a little more about each other and sharing emotional snippets, and there seems to be an increasing connection between us. I wonder how Cheryl plans to spend the afternoon. "A yoga class," she says. I scrunch my nose. I have never done yoga and I prefer to spend the afternoon in the sun. "Perhaps we can meet later for a walk on the beach? Meet you by the pool about 8pm?" She nods, kisses my cheek and goes off to practise her poses and stretches.

I walk to my favourite beach near the swimming pool, all sparkling white sand and gorgeous aquamarine water. The views here are spectacular so I sit on my towel and stare at the ocean for a while.

I am getting the hang of being more present, and it's not that hard really. I leave my book to one side and start to notice everything around me, paying attention to what I am hearing and seeing and feeling. I notice my breathing. As usual, everything seems to slow down and I arrive at a serene and expansive frame of mind.

The more I am present with What Is Happening Now, the less I am aware of time. I am also noticing the disappearance of regret, anxiety and worry. I surmise that those feelings belong to the past and the future, and there is no space for them when I am fully present in the Moment.

There is only Now. The past and future are merely a dream. You can use your Now to learn from the past and to plan your future but as soon as the learning and planning are complete, return to the Now. All of Life is contained in the Now.

How does he do that? I cannot see him anywhere on the beach. I gaze across the waves and spot a long-haired, dark-skinned guy riding a kitesurfer. Aha! Jay looks in my direction, whoops joyfully, and starts an impossibly slow 360 degree loop high in the air. Time seems to stand still. Some people on the beach are clapping and cheering. It's not just me then. Not an illusion inside my head!

Everything is Now. Keep practising Awareness and Presence. Notice every bird – the ones coming in through your senses and the ones inside your mind. They are all birds in your sky.

I am practising ... but you are some kind of miracle-worker far beyond the rest of us.

Your birds – thoughts, words, labels, judgements, conditions, stories – these all create a barrier between you and others, between you and Reality, between you and Life.

I don't completely understand these meditation teachings. How can I fly or walk on water or heal people? Jay is a fair distance away out on the ocean and I can feel his penetrating gaze from here. He lets the kite go and it flutters wildly for a few moments. He is just standing out at sea, looking at me. I feel the hairs on my neck standing up. The air around me feels weird.

Jay extends a hand and the entire beach hears: "I SAY YOU ARE FREE!"

People are looking at *me* now. I feel uncomfortable. I do not want another mob incident. I certainly don't need this attention. There is no way I am going out there. I grab my towel and run. Sorry, Jay, I will be free another day.

I soon find myself at a very quiet beach on the side of the island near the workers' residence. A little shop is selling snorkelling gear and clothing and I decide to hide in here for a while. The man behind the counter looks at me with a hint of recognition. "You are the ice-cream vendor, aren't you?" I enquire, trying to keep my breathing calm. I wonder what kind of world I have entered.

"It's scary when you start discovering your true nature," he says, gently smiling. He gestures with his head: "Come on ..." He locks the shop and we wander down to the boat jetty and sit on a strip of beach.

"If you choose to believe your current identity and stay where you are, no worries. But if you want to move forward and discover your true nature, you may have to lose some of your illusions. That's going to hurt a bit."

Part of me intuitively understands what he means. I feel a struggle within me, like I am bridging two worlds and I cannot see the way forward. How will life be on the other side?

I am Evan. He bursts out laughing at the look on my face. *Yes, of course I can speak inside your mind!* I smile and shake my head; why on earth am I surprised?

Let me tell you about your life as it is now. Your body knows only transitory pleasures: one day you have a great meal, the next day you are hungry; one morning the sun shines warmly on your skin, in the afternoon it rains and the wind blows coldly. You strive to maximise the Pleasure that your body can experience but it is like owning a car – you have to keep putting in fuel. It's unending.

Your mind strives in the same way to attain Happiness. You try to control events, situations and people in order to maximise your happiness. But your happiness comes and goes – the romantic partner who gives you great joy today is the source of your irritation and pain just a few months later. A great job diminishes into a boring routine. Your happiness ebbs and flows, and you never arrive at a point of complete happiness.

Do you know why this situation exists?

I am searching the library of my mind. There is a glimmer in the corner and a book seems to fall open. Ah! "The body and mind both depend on gratification from the outside. They can only be satisfied by external sources."

Excellent! Your body-mind is a slave to everything outside of you. It depends on food, water, air, praise, recognition, affection, nurturing and emotional connection. It is forever chasing these but never seems to be satisfied. And how can it be? The body-mind is like a black hole continually drawing in as much light as it can, yet it never gets filled.

I have to agree. The more of life I experience, the more I realise that nothing ever truly fulfils, and nothing ever satisfies for long. This often leaves me with an emptiness inside and sometimes this emptiness leads to anxiety, frustration and sadness. I recall the numerous times I have said to myself: Why can't I be happy? Why can't it all just fall into place?

The weird thing is that a solid education, business success and status have made no difference to my long-term happiness. I just feel a thrill for a while, or a burst of joy, and then it subsides to an itch that never gets fully scratched. It seems that nothing fails like success.

Helping other people feels good at the time, whether through therapy or a kind act, but this happiness also diminishes. Being in a loving relationship gives me lots of pleasure but not an enduring deep inner joy. I wonder what it feels like to have children …

This underlying emptiness in each one of you leads to anxiety and fear and depression and greed. It also results in the need to possess, the need for attachment, and the need for control, and even generates a sense of entitlement (I deserve this or that). Imagine a world where these things do not exist!

"Evan, I give up. What's the answer then?"

For a long while he studies the small island across the water. *You are not your body-mind. As long as you identify with it, you will always experience this emptiness and never be truly satisfied or happy. And your planet will continue on its path of exploitation, greed and misery.*

"Then what am I?" I ask softly.

This is exactly what you are discovering. What Jay is hinting at with his mysterious teachings. When you discover your true nature, you will know that you are free.

"You are starting to sound like Jay now," I mutter impatiently. "You must have gone to the same cryptic school."

Here is a clue: The body knows fleeting pleasure, the mind knows fleeting happiness, the heart knows fleeting joy, and Awareness knows enduring Bliss.

Evan stands up, places his hand on my shoulder and flashes a big smile. He walks away to his beach shop, leaving me to ponder the mystery. I look for his footprints in the sand. A cool breeze flutters the leaves behind me. If I am not my body-mind ... then what am I?

I have this sudden urge to run. I pick myself up and gallop along the secluded beach shouting gibberish at the top of my voice. I don't care. My brain is overloaded. I dance and make unintelligible noises and kick sand everywhere. After about twenty minutes I collapse on my back, exhausted. My eyes close and I sink into absolute silence and something incredible happens. Inside of me is nothing, emptiness, silence, but the Silence feels like another dimension and the Emptiness a doorway into another world. I am lying here sensing something I have never felt before, something indescribable flowing from that place of nothingness inside me ... and it's a deep serenity ... it's bliss.

When I open my eyes, the world seems different. I have been following a trail of inscrutable clues all the way down the rabbit hole. I am not sure how I got here or whether I can stay or what it all means. I feel acutely aware of ... Emptiness. My senses are heightened. I am walking in slow motion and feeling connected with everything around me. The palm trees seem alive and I vividly sense their energy. The ocean whooshes around me and I can't separate myself from the rolling waves. I am in the centre of Everything and know a Silence that I cannot define or express.

I feel a thump on my chest and hear a voice say: "Get out of the way, you idiot!" Ah, a story. One hand clapping. I bend down and pick up the neon-green flying disc and it feels strangely alive in my hand. I know I can send this flying disc to its destination purely by intention, and after the tiniest gesture it makes an acutely slow and huge arc back to its astounded owner.

Is this my true nature? What does it all mean? Maybe Evan is making sense after all. I feel delighted and a rush of soft energy flows through me. I sit down at a restaurant table near the beach and feel enchanted by the soft waves. A crimson sun slides gently beneath the mauve ocean and it's incredibly beautiful. About an hour passes and my sense of bliss slowly subsides.

I stroll over to the pool to meet Cheryl. I am looking forward to seeing her. It's a full moon and, although the beach is a bit dark, the sea is lit up like a theatre waiting for a play to commence.

It's all smiles, and she hooks her arm into mine as we amble along the warm sand. We chat about our passions, our loves, our hopes, our dreams. I like Cheryl very much. It is so comfortable being with her. I can sense a friendship forming and this is important to me. While I may need a solid foundation of honesty and integrity in a relationship, I especially need strong cornerstones of friendship and loving-kindness.

For a moment we stand and gaze at the moon above the palms. Everything is bathed in a silvery light. I have a warm feeling in my chest and my tummy is tingling. I turn quietly and look intently into Cheryl's inviting brown eyes. I take her in my arms and my hand gently embraces the nape under her soft curls. I sense her breathing quickening. I linger near her sensual lips and her soft scent plays a sweet song in my head. We kiss slowly, longingly, lovingly, passionately. It is dizzying and dreamy.

The moon dances a playful pirouette across her face. She is so beautiful. We tumble onto the luminous sand like intertwined pussycats and then cuddle together and gaze at the polished cobalt blue ocean. There is no need for words. We both know something very special is beginning.

* * *

It is morning and I am sitting on a fluffy towel on the beach, just watching. The sea air is invigorating and my breathing is calm and deep. I am noticing the gentle spray of the waves, the fresh breeze fluttering the palms and the new sun rippling gold across the ocean.

I am witnessing my thoughts – these lively birds that fly across my sky. Some are noisy and intrusive like gulls fighting for scraps and some are sneaky and quiet like a kite hovering high and watching its prey. That intensely alive and expansive feeling comes over me and I enter deep silence and peace. I sense a profound connection to everything.

Nice awareness, Steve. Jay walks over and sits next to me. *I think you're getting the hang of this.*

"Jay, it's kind of weird. I am on a beach in the middle of the ocean, far away from Western business and busyness, and I have nothing here, yet I feel so peaceful and filled up."

Has it occurred to you that you will lose everything eventually?

"What do you mean?"

No matter how hard you work, how much money you save, how cleverly you invest, and how many possessions you have, you will lose everything in the end. You will age and your body will change. One day you will be on your death-bed and you will face the reality of losing it all. Everything.

"What's your point?"

What is really important? What will you take with you in the end? What, at this moment, is lacking?

"Um ... I really don't know."

Let's go wakeboarding! Jay seems energised and enthusiastic, and the ocean is calm, so I jump on one of the bicycles he has brought with him. We cycle across the island, hire wetsuits and wait for the boat to arrive. I remind Jay that I have not wakeboarded before.

It's like waterskiing, except both feet are on one mini-surfboard. Very much like snowboarding. The motorboat will tow you and you just ride the wakes left by the boat. It's good fun.

So here I am submerged in the water with a board strapped to my feet, holding the tow rope handle. Jay is on the boat beaming a huge smile at me. What's up with him? The boat starts slowly moving and now I feel this huge pressure as the wakeboard encounters the resistance of the water. Something has to give and soon I am being dragged across the surface of the water. I let go the handle and the boat stops. Jay is laughing wildly. *Try angling the board up a bit more!*

Soon the water pushes hard against my thighs and after a few more collapsed attempts I finally have lift-off. Getting out of the water is the hardest part. Once I am on the surface I manage to board for a few seconds before I hit the water. After a few more attempts I am moving across the wakes behind the boat. Each time I stay on the board longer and it gets a little easier.

Once you understand the basic technique, you keep expanding it. Everything is just an extension of the initial technique. Get out of the water and surf the wakes, surf the wakes, surf the wakes. Get out of your mind and watch the birds, watch the birds, watch the birds.

After an hour, we return to the beach and feast on tropical fruit. We drink lots of water and lay in the sun for a while. I am thinking about Jay's words. It's true – the hardest part is getting out of the water ... after that it gets easier and easier.

After lunch it is Jay's turn. I wonder if he even needs a tow rope. Jay is in the water, the boat moves, and he gets up easily and smoothly. He seems so serene as he executes perfect arcs across the water and a few slow jumps in the air. I am watching him and it looks surreal, as if he is blending with the air and the water and the tow rope. What on earth is he doing?

Not doing, Steve. Being.

I remember the levitating monks in Bhutan. What was it they said? *It is not about doing, rather about being. When you do, you cannot be. When you be, you can do anything.*

There is something so close to me, so near my consciousness, but just out of reach. When will I wake up and finally get it? Perhaps this Being state gives you access to anything ... I wonder if Being is the acceptance of every possibility.

I am looking at Jay. He is still on the surface of the water but he is no longer holding the tow rope. The boat is not moving; in fact nothing is moving. Everything is in freeze-frame. There is just Jay and me and a white light getting brighter around us. *What was that, Steve?*

"Being is the acceptance of every possibility." My voice seems to echo bizarrely and I wonder where we are.

Excellent! Being is the acceptance of every possibility. How does it look in here?

"Where are we? Everything is white. There is nothing but light."

Where do you want to be?

For a nanosecond I think of Cheryl and instantly there is scenery and I am on the beach near the water bungalows and Cheryl is walking up ahead. Wow, there was not even a shimmer. "Are you still there, Jay?"

There is only Here and Now, and everything is a Thought of Life. Enjoy your afternoon.

It's simply too much to process. I amble up to Cheryl. She greets me in her usual enthusiastic manner with a warm smile. "Hey," I say, and give her a big hug.

"Where did you appear from?" she asks. I rub my chin thoughtfully. "It's funny you should ask ..." I tell her about the day's activities. "Honestly, Cheryl, I feel like a student getting a D-grade. I don't know what to make of it all. Do you think I will ever understand everything?"

She giggles. "I practise radical acceptance: Acceptance of Reality As It Is."

"Wow, where did you learn that?"

"There is this guy called Evan and we chat every so often. He owns a couple of motorcycle and bicycle shops in Tuscany. I saw him yesterday actually."

I groan. Not *the* Evan surely! Have I been scripted into some great cosmic play?

"Evan says that whatever passes through my mind, I need only watch it come and go, lightly and without attachment. I no longer try to block my thoughts and feelings or chase after them. I simply observe them, as if they are all just passing through."

"That's awesome, Cheryl."

"Radical acceptance is also about saying Yes to Life: Yes to whatever Life brings. I have found this idea the most challenging. Evan has a mantra: 'Accept then Act.' It means that you accept what Life brings to you, try not to hold on to what is presented, and then take action that you deem appropriate. Radical acceptance, non-attachment, action. It makes sense but I don't always get it right." She glances down at the sand for a moment.

"Meditation is simply compassionate awareness of my thoughts and feelings, and compassionate awareness of others' thoughts and feelings, and finally compassionate awareness of the situations and events that Life brings across my path." She smiles, looking a little proud of herself.

I have never met anyone like Cheryl. I grab her around the waist, look into her eyes and passionately kiss her. "Just because you're you," I say.

We spend the rest of the day relaxing on the beach, exchanging amusing personal stories, giggling on our backs at the cloud formations and silently gazing over the gorgeous aquamarine sea. We manage to spend a lovely afternoon in a perfectly useless manner.

We have dinner at our favourite restaurant, Ristorante Al Pontile, which serves traditional Italian cuisine and Japanese specialties and has splendid views over the ocean. It is decorated with Italian-inspired art so Cheryl feels right at home.

After our sumptuous dessert, Cheryl reaches across the table and lays her hand on mine: "I am leaving in a few days." It is a poignant gesture and I understand immediately. I raise my glass of Chianti: "To new love, Cheryl. We will find a way to be together." She clinks my glass and there is a sense of relief in her eyes.

The next few days we are inseparable. Jay is nowhere to be found so I invite Cheryl to stay at the water bungalow. My bed is huge and we become entangled in fluffy pillow fights, long wet kisses and cosy candlelight cuddles. We spend luscious champagne evenings naked in the hot tub immersed in glorious instrumental music. We have long conversations and deep silences as we gaze across the moonlit ocean.

We awaken to fruit-filled breakfasts on the sun-drenched patio, then splash about in the shallow water near the bungalow, laughing like carefree children. We charter a small boat and our guide takes us snorkelling on a private coral reef. We lunch romantically on a remote island. We hold hands and dream and laugh and cry.

It is our last night together and we make love for the first time. Cheryl lights a dozen candles and soft music plays in the background. The whoosh of the sea intertwines with the moonlight and caresses our naked bodies. We make love slowly and languidly, sensually stroking and exploring every inch of skin, our eyes dancing over each other, our bitter-sweet thoughts of tomorrow gradually abandoned to the rise and fall of a distant ocean.

For a long while we lay gently in each other's arms, like two butterflies replete with nectar. Then the night tenderly kisses our eyelids and we drift into blissful sleep.

* * *

I am staring at the cascade of Cheryl's hair across the white pillow. I would like to awaken to this vision every day of my life. She rouses and says: "Promise me there will be no tears. This is not goodbye. It is only until we see each other again." I nod.

I invite her into my arms and hold her close. "I love you, Cheryl." Our eyes meet. She looks so vulnerable and open for a moment. I caress her face and gently kiss her. I pretend not to notice the happy tear squeeze its way to freedom.

And then she is away, and I am left with a postcard and carefully recorded contact details.

I spend the rest of the morning alone on the patio, staring at the sea. I am not in the mood for company. I *will* see her again but right now it feels like someone has dimmed the lights. I lunch alone at the water bungalow. In the afternoon I take a long swim in the undulating sea.

In the evening Jay arrives at the bungalow along with a chef who cooks and serves a delicious meal. I am starving and deeply grateful. We dine inside as the wind has picked up. Jay doesn't say a word. He knows better than to try to soothe my gloomy heart. After dinner he pours me a glass of wine. I notice that it's a Chianti. He raises a glass, smiles kindly, and toasts: "To new love."

* * *

For the remaining two weeks in the Maldives, Jay and I take long walks on the beaches and discuss life, the universe and everything. It is a very peaceful time, and possibly one of the best places in the world to be discussing such deep and interesting topics. Jay is incredibly kind and patient and I guess he has been a great teacher to many people.

We are sitting under the palm trees at the water's edge with mangos, pawpaw and watermelon. Jay is staring out over the ocean. He sighs. *A long time ago, we used to live side by side with humans on this earth. Many of you still remember that era.*

As you have seen, as soon as we allowed a miracle or healing, everything changed. Chaos usually ensued. So we learned to keep a low profile and blend in with the local population. We tried to walk quietly on this earth and teach the simple truths of loving-kindness and responsibility for each other and the planet.

A few of us became kings and rulers, shaping cultures and teaching relatively advanced knowledge. We built Stonehenge in England and some of the Egyptian pyramids and the Easter Island statues. We drew the lines on the ground in Nazca, Peru. We left our mark all over this planet.

Unfortunately, technological prowess among our peoples often exceeded spiritual development and there were clashes. Our involvement, though well intentioned, was having dangerous consequences. We decided that humans needed autonomy and self-determination, free from our advanced technology.

We vowed never to rule on your planet, and many of us withdrew to teach on other worlds. Sadly, once we withdrew from your world most of our teachings were bent and corrupted. Men formed religions to influence and control vast populations. Power and greed took over, and the teachings of loving-kindness and responsibility for each other and the planet were forsaken.

"Is this connected to some of the myths and mysteries in our history, and to the archaeological discoveries that have uncovered strange and challenging findings?"

Yes ... There are very few of us left on the earth now. We tread quietly and teach the same truths. Soon, however, there will be a return of many of the teachers. Your planet is in a dire state and is slowly being destroyed. A few million people own and control the world's resources while billions are starving or living in appalling conditions, and most of you seem to stand by and watch. Greed and power are reaching their terrible climax and love is seldom seen.

"I know. The world is in a miserable predicament and it seems to be getting worse."

Jay looks at me with a twinkle in his eye. *There are people trying to make a difference in all spheres of life. Political activists, social workers, nurses and doctors working in poor countries, people donating to charities, professionals doing pro bono work, and those who spread ideas – the teachers.*

I am munching sliced watermelon and trying to digest all of Jay's words. There are a few pips and I spit them out but overall it is good melon and I thoroughly enjoy it. He looks at me kindly, his metallic blue eyes shining: *Our time is coming to an end, Steve. For now.*

I feel a bit panicky. First Cheryl, now Jay! "What do you mean? Where will you go?"

There is a change coming to your planet and there are many who need my teachings. Keep practising what you have learned. The teachings are simple. The rest is up to you. Awareness ... consciousness ... noticing ... being the witness of your thoughts, feelings and experiences.

"Yeah, yeah. Watch the birds, I know." I reflect for a moment. "Will you be there when I need you? If I have questions? If I get stuck?"

If you think my name, I will know. We interact on many dimensions beyond this physical reality.

We share a big hug, then Jay begins to shimmer and fade away. "When will I see you again?" I shout into the pale image. *When you are ready, Steve ...*

I feel reality biting. Paradise suddenly feels like a lonely place.

I have two more days before I fly home so I spend the time meditating on the gorgeous beaches, snorkelling in the azure waters and having luxurious massages at the spa. I exchange a couple of emails with Cheryl and it's good to hear that she misses me.

I have my last supper at the restaurant where we met and watch the splendid sunset. There is much to ponder – my future with Cheryl, the enigma of Jay, and the profound and mystical teachings. I feel despondent and alone but also excited and deeply appreciative of everything I have experienced in the Maldives.

Tuscany, Italy

I am relaxing at the London therapy centre, reclining on my black leather chair. On the opposite wall there is a large photo of the Maldivian water bungalows with an ocean backdrop. I find myself drifting away, lost in sweet memories of those awesome beaches, swaying palms and incredible sapphire waters. I miss the gorgeous massages, the mouth-watering fruit platters and the lazy chats in the warm sunshine.

Cheryl and I phone each other every day. Even with the flurry of emails, I am finding that a long-distance relationship can be lonely and frustrating. We meet up for a few days in London and it is fun and romantic and passionate, yet tainted with impending heartache. We both bury ourselves in our busy schedules and manage a couple more days here and there. It is already July when Cheryl invites me to Tuscany for ten days in early September. I buy my plane ticket the same day.

The weeks pass by in slow motion and I have plenty of time to witness all my thoughts and feelings. Jay is probably somewhere in the world smiling at me right now. At least I am practising all I have learned. Interestingly, many people are making comments about my demeanour: "You seem so much calmer these days" or "You seem more relaxed and happy".

The truth is I *am* noticing differences in me. My heart feels more open to others; my intuition and awareness seem lucid and expansive; and I am responding to people and events calmly and spontaneously. The best thing is that my bouts of anxiety have been slowly replaced by wonderful feelings of well-being and confidence. I understand why Jay said it was time for him to leave and for me to practise the teachings.

Occasionally I share with clients a little of what Jay has taught me. I am no expert in Jay's concepts and sometimes I feel I have no idea what I am talking about. Yet many of my regular clients are experiencing significant increases in peace, happiness and well-being. So maybe there is something to all his mumbo-jumbo after all.

At last the day arrives to fly to Tuscany. Part of me expects to see Jay in the airport. It's been months since I saw or heard from him. And my life of miracles has settled into the ordinary routine of everyday life. I am not complaining. I am happier than I have ever been. And I am in love!

* * *

I arrive at Florence Airport (Aeroporto di Firenze) and finally enter Cheryl's world with a huge embrace and kiss. We dance around like two reunited puppies. She hooks her arm into mine in her customary way and we find a taxi and are soon heading to her apartment. Florence is a beautiful Italian city and I am looking forward to seeing it all.

Cheryl's apartment is a fabulous aristocratic three-bedroom affair on the top floor of an old building. The ceilings are high and the front room is more window than wall which creates an awesome feeling of space in what is already a vast room. The front room decor is an eclectic mix of brown leather sofa, a couple of chaise longues, a wingback chair and two recliners all vaguely surrounding an enormous glass coffee table. A velvet bench runs along one of the walls, scattered with purple and mauve cushions, just begging for a glass of wine and a gaze across the magnificent views of the city.

Polished oak floorboards run through the apartment, covered here and there by rugs. The warm kitchen looks exactly as I imagine an Italian kitchen – all rustic terracotta, olive oil and pasta. The bedrooms are far smaller than the rest of the house and have been individually fashioned in the old-world style of the medieval and Renaissance periods. The bathroom is Italian tile from floor to ceiling with a gorgeous all-glass shower large enough to bathe a small elephant.

"I inherited this place from my parents five years ago when they retired to the countryside. And I gradually redecorated each room into its own unique style. It is a beautiful apartment but the rates and taxes are ridiculous."

"I love it, Cheryl. It feels like your home."

We settle on the brown leather sofa. Cheryl has prepared a light meal of affettati misti (cold sliced meats) arranged in a circle and decorated with crisp, tangy salad leaves, along with thick slices of bread and extra virgin olive oil for dipping. And, as she kindly explains, a young and fairly light Chianti to keep us company.

We spend the afternoon relaxing in her warm apartment, catching up on each other's news, and generally being silly and in love. There is Italian classical music in the background and the sun is glimmering through the windows. Everything is peaceful and content in our world.

In the evening I offer to take Cheryl out to dinner. Enjoying great food and excellent wine in Florence is not difficult at all, as there seems to be a trattoria or ristorante down almost every street. Cheryl steers us to her favourite trattoria. As I soon learn, a trattoria is less formal than a ristorante. There are generally no printed menus, the service is casual, and wine is sold by the decanter rather than the bottle. Prices are reasonable and the food is usually regional and local.

The sound of Italian flowing off Cheryl's tongue turns my brain into honey. It is a romantic, passionate, musical language and I am sitting in the middle of a finely tuned orchestra. We share ravioli nudi, which has a stuffing of spinach, ricotta, eggs, grated Parmesan, flour and a pinch of nutmeg; followed by pollo alla fiorentina, a heavenly concoction of chicken breasts with bread crumbs, Parmesan cheese, spinach, onion, celery, cream cheese, paprika and garlic powder. The food is beyond words.

Somewhere between Cheryl's Italian, her gorgeous eyes, the superb wine and the scrumptious food, I become quite intoxicated. She is not far behind. Later we stumble home and make glorious, passionate love in her Renaissance room and then fall asleep curled in each other's arms.

The next day, after a rather slow start, Cheryl takes me on a romantic walking tour of Florence. It is more sensible to hire a bicycle or take a walk as most streets are pedestrian-only and the main historic centre is relatively small with scarce parking.

Florence is at the heart of the Italian Renaissance and it feels like we are walking in an open-air museum of piazzas and historical buildings. Cheryl explains that Florence's cathedrals, churches and palaces were designed, built and decorated by many of the most illustrious artists of the time, from Brunelleschi to

Michelangelo. Many of the main squares display statues by Giambologna or Michelangelo. We visit two museums and a few churches and chapels and find magnificent paintings, sculptures and frescoes created by some of the greatest minds of all time. Is it possible to fall in love with a city?

As a superb finale, Cheryl introduces me to a local gelateria with its wide range of colours and flavours. My gelato has me singing falsettos. The shop owner proudly points out that gelato is not Italian *ice cream* but would be better defined as *ice milk*, as the Italians have found that too much butterfat interferes with the transfer of fresh flavours to the tongue. I love these Italians.

My limited knowledge of Italians had me imagining all verbose rambling and fiery body language. In truth, they are ordinary people, warm and friendly and helpful. Cheryl, in particular, never seems to get her feathers ruffled. She is decisive, passionate and straight-talking but she also seems so calm and centred, even when she is harassed by loud flirtations or the hoots of a motorcycle that swerves close to us.

Tonight is a relaxing evening in the apartment. We are making a simple pasta dish in her warm kitchen and I am getting an education in Italian opera. It's the full immersion experience and I am as yet unsure whether I will be adding this genre to my music collection.

When dinner quietens to Italian instrumental music, and the candlelight is casting soft shadows across the dinner table, I wonder aloud about Cheryl's calm nature. "I was not always like this," she smiles, and her eyes flit away for a moment. "Do you remember Evan, global purveyor of goods and part-time spiritual teacher?" I nod and we burst into laughter.

She continues: "He has some strange teachings. He told me once that I am nothing but a wave rolling on the ocean of life. And that other people are rolling waves too. As waves, we rise up from the endless ocean, create some white foam and noisy splashes, and then we dissolve back into the ocean.

"He asked why I take everything and everyone so seriously. We are all part of the same ocean, even though each wave appears different and sounds unique. Why not let each wave just *be*, and if I am fully Present with a particular wave it will fulfil its purpose and then subside."

I am listening and trying to keep up. "It's definitely the cryptic school of philosophy. How does anyone completely understand these teachings?"

"I have no idea. I am still trying to work this one out: Evan says that wise people have no fixed mind and don't know who they are; also they don't collect precious things and don't hold on to ideas. Say what?" She shrugs her shoulders and breaks into a fit of giggles.

"I do like his advice to drift like a wave on the ocean. We are all waves and if I try to hold onto another person or try to control or change them in some way – they will simply slip through my fingers and continue their journey.

"So now I allow myself to be me – flowing my way through the ocean – and I allow others to flow their way through the ocean. I am I and You are You, and if by chance we dance well together … that's wonderful; if not, I am free to flow away."

"That's beautiful, Cheryl. I think you are becoming a sage." Her eyes are twinkling in the diffuse light and she looks so peaceful and content.

"You know, one of the greatest gifts of Evan's teachings is my sense of freedom. I am now less concerned with others' opinions and comments. People who focus on others tend to project their stories and see only *who they themselves are*. How can you enter a relationship of any kind when you only see reflections of yourself? Then you cannot truly *see the other person*.

"So *my* freedom has set others free too. Because I allow others to just *be*, because I accept others *as they are*, I am now able to be truly open and Present with others, and for the first time I really understand how to Listen.

"I have learned that the greatest gift I can give to others is being completely Present in the Moment and truly Listening to who they are and what they say. No labels, judgements or agendas, and none of my stories – just Being with the other person."

I am enthralled. Is Evan teaching me through Cheryl? The music has stopped and the atmosphere feels quiet and divine. Cheryl goes to change the music and I nip to the washroom. In the hallway is a framed Rumi print and I notice in beautiful calligraphy: 'You are not just a drop in the ocean. You are the mighty ocean in a drop.'

It has been a long day and soon we are reading in bed. We fall asleep curled up together under a light blanket like two children who are best friends.

* * *

It is a joy to awaken and see Cheryl's bright smile and ruffled hair. I wish every morning could be like this. I pull the blanket up over me and drift into thinking about us. About how we can be together. About the future. I feel my heart stir strongly. I love this woman and I want to be with her.

As if sensing my thoughts, she snuggles in close to me and places her head on my chest. "Why don't we have an easy day today? Perhaps a little shopping and a light lunch out. There are some lovely shops I can show you." I stroke her hair affectionately for a while. "That sounds good to me, sweetheart."

I pad out of the bedroom and into the glorious shower. I swear it echoes when you sing. I am feeling ebullient and I draw little hearts all over the huge glass doors. Cheryl comes in and giggles: "You silly crazy-in-love man!" She joins me under the waterfall and kisses me passionately. Warm rivulets pour over our naked bodies and gentle billows of steam hug us. The deep wet kisses make my tummy tingle.

I slowly and carefully dry Cheryl's moist body ... my fingers linger lusciously ... our tongues caress each other in a raw and sexy dance. She wraps her legs around me. Outside the window we hear the peal of church bells reaching a fervent crescendo.

Soon we are dressed and out the door and holding hands like young lovers in the streets of romantic Florence. Cheryl is gaily inviting me into luxury boutiques, craft shops, antique stores and artists' studios. Open-air food markets offer a range of delicious meats, wines, fruit and cheese, and I sample everything on offer. Tuscany appears to be a gastronomic heaven.

Over a late lunch of tasty soup with chunks of fresh bread, Cheryl the tour guide announces: "I would like to show you more of

Tuscany than just Florence. This may be our regional capital but we have beautiful cities like Lucca and Vinci and Chianti and Siena. We also have six World Heritage Sites: the historic centres of Florence and San Gimignano and Siena and Pienza, the square of the Cathedral of Pisa, and the Val d'Orcia. And we have over one hundred-and-twenty protected nature reserves."

She gives me a penetrating gaze. We have not yet discussed the idea of living together. Perhaps she is hoping that a grand tour of Tuscany will add a piece to this puzzle. I place my hands on hers and look into her eyes: "I love Florence, Cheryl. And I really appreciate you showing me around." She smiles and sighs softly.

On our way back I purchase a bouquet of flowers and I see Cheryl's face light up. The stall manager winks at me and smiles broadly: "The Italians *we love flowers!*" As we amble home through the Florentine streets, I place my arm around her waist and sing "I love you!"

* * *

In the morning we decide to take the train to Lucca, a city completely encircled by massively thick sixteenth-century Roman walls. It's a couple of hours away and an opportunity to view the magnificent Tuscan countryside.

We walk the short distance from Lucca station to one of the city entrances. A few minutes later we drop our bags at a small hotel just off a huge square lined with shops and restaurants. Cheryl grabs my hand and soon we arrive at a bicycle shop. And there in a back room, hands covered in grease, with The Beach Boys song 'Wouldn't It Be Nice' blaring in the background, is Evan.

"I was wondering when you'd get here!" he shouts enthusiastically over the noise. Evan has a deep tan and a huge grin and I feel like I have arrived in sunny California. He leaves the upside-down bicycle and comes bounding over. In the instant he reaches to hug Cheryl, I notice his hands are miraculously clean. Ah, we are back in the land of the surreal. He gives me a big hug. "How are you two?" he asks, smiling kindly.

I shrug and smile and let Cheryl chat with him for a while. After half an hour Evan scurries away and returns with two gleaming bicycles and some basic instructions, and then he waves us away: "See you later, kids. Have fun!"

Cheryl guides us up a paved ramp that leads onto the city wall. The wall is wider than a single-lane street and has been converted into an avenue lined with trees. People are walking, jogging and cycling up here. What a fantastic idea! We cycle around the entire city enjoying the panoramic views, then dip down another ramp to explore the fine medieval and Renaissance architecture, great restaurants and antique markets within the city walls.

Lucca is known as the town of one hundred churches. It is a real gem, with quaint narrow lanes zigzagging the city and offering a mouth-watering array of shops, wine bars, bakeries and restaurants. After two pleasurable days of touring the city, we return the bicycles and arrange for Evan to join us for dinner.

Tonight is the Festival of Lights, known locally as Luminaria di Santa Croce. The focal point of the festival is a wooden sculpture of Christ housed inside the Lucca cathedral. Everyone turns off their lights and candles are placed in all the windows. The city looks spectacular. Later, a long procession of priests and clergy moves through the town, accompanied by a marching band.

Now there was a man who gave up his life for Love. Who made the ultimate sacrifice. Who paid the ultimate price to enter the kingdom of Heaven.

We are supping an excellent wine in a trattoria just off the main path of the procession. Cheryl looks up at Evan, a little surprised. "I didn't know you were religious. What do you mean?"

There are only two paths to enlightenment: Love and Awareness. He chose Love and came Home.

As usual, I am a little lost. Cheryl is just listening, completely focused on Evan.

To truly Love you have to die to your self; to be fully Aware you will lose everything and find emptiness. Two paths, same destination. Either way, your consciousness enters the kingdom of Heaven. You come Home.

I am trying really hard to focus. The candles are flickering softly and Evan's words seem to be slowly echoing in my mind.

Love has different degrees and stages, each one drawing you deeper like a moth to a flame until you are completely burned and no longer exist. You become Love. You are Love.

Awareness is like water: transparent, flowing, yielding, empty, hard to grasp. When you look for Awareness, there is nothing to see; when you listen for it, there is nothing to hear.

"Evan, what are you teaching us?" I ask.

I am not teaching you. You are Consciousness and you are listening to yourself.

Then Evan beams his award-winning smile and packs up in a fit of laughter. Cheryl and I watch him, bemused. When he comes to, his saintly question is: "What's for dessert?"

The rest of the evening is spent in great mirth; the desserts are superb and the wine flows merrily into midnight. I have this strange thought that Evan is blessing our romantic relationship. Finally, there are hugs all round and Evan departs for his bicycle shop with a friendly salute: "See you in the morning."

As we walk away I muse about Evan's plentiful smiles and laughter. In the background there is a faint giggle like the rustling of leaves: *From Here, Steve, the illusion looks hilarious and it's hard to take it seriously. You will understand in time.*

I place my arm across Cheryl's shoulders and touch my head to hers: "I love sharing these days with you." Soon we are asleep, and in my dreams we are playing and kissing in a misty blue lake with invisible shores.

In the morning we collect a motorcycle from Evan for the short trip to Pisa. We could go by train but we like the idea of romantically touring Italy on a scooter. Soon we are weaving through the Tuscan traffic and I am intently practising Presence and Awareness.

There is a lot more to see than the Leaning Tower of Pisa and the Piazza dei Miracoli (Square of Miracles). Pisa offers a selection of palaces, churches, museums, Gothic buildings and the bridges across the River Arno, so the time passes rather quickly.

By the end of the day we are both tired and hungry, so we race back to Lucca for a hearty dinner and some downtime. We spend a relaxing evening at the hotel absorbed in our books. Tomorrow we will catch the train back to Florence.

* * *

It is really good to be back in Cheryl's apartment and we spend the entire day doing nothing. I am staring out the window imagining a possible life in Florence. What would I do for a living? Not much work here for an English psychotherapist. Italian is a beautiful language and I will have to learn it. All these possibilities are running circles in my mind.

"Where are your parents, Cheryl?" I ask her over lunch. "You mentioned that they are retired?"

"They live an hour away in Vinci on a farm with a vineyard and olive trees. It is hard work so my brother and his wife manage the farm. About five years ago this apartment was put into my name and the farm into my brother's name – a kind of early inheritance. At the same time they converted part of the farm into an agriturismo.

"Mother is an amazing cook and father is a vigneron but he sells his grapes to a winemaker. Our rustic agriturismo has seven guest bedrooms, an outside swimming pool and farmland in all directions. Vinci is a small town but there are nice restaurants and the museum of Leonardo da Vinci is in the town centre. Did you know he was born in Vinci?"

I shake my head and smile. My heart feels warm. I love the way her eyes sparkle when she talks animatedly.

"Cheryl, I want to share my life with you. We need to talk about how we can do this. Is it too soon to discuss?"

She jumps up, knocking over her chair, and throws her arms around me and squeals. "It's not too soon!"

So we spend the next hour throwing ideas into the air. She works in New York, London and Florence. Her apartment is stunning. I love Florence. I can't speak Italian. How can I work as a therapist here? How much time can she spend in London? How will we cope with time apart? Where should we live? What do we want out of life?

We crack open a bottle of Brunello di Montalcino and we are hummingbirds supping nectar, all ideas and questions and delight and anticipation and I feel alive and aware of every sound and then everything slows down and becomes really still and peaceful and I can tell that she feels it too and we both hear the soft whisper: *Everything is going to be fine.*

I lean forward and kiss her gently. There is so much heart connection between us. She looks at me for a few moments. "I want you to meet my parents before you go back to London. How about tomorrow?" There is a moment of apprehension but I nod in agreement. It's time to meet the parents. I refresh the wine glasses.

* * *

Cheryl is driving and I am marvelling at the endless parades of sunflowers, vineyards and olive trees. The sun is shining brightly and the sky is the lightest blue. There is a constant whirring and whoosh as packs of professional cyclists whizz past. Vinci is a rural town surrounded by Tuscan hills and it looks like a pleasant place for a rustic vacation.

We drive directly into the town centre and visit the Museo Leonardiano (museum of Leonardo da Vinci) which displays many of his drawings and models. The museum is quite interesting and afterwards we stand for a while on the castle rampart and gaze over the charming scenery. We have lunch down the road at a lovely open-air restaurant surrounded by ivy-covered trellises.

A little later we are parking the car in the pebbled driveway of the agriturismo. It's all quiet and suddenly I hear a shriek and it's a flurry of people. Cheryl's parents, her brother, his wife and two children are exchanging hugs and kisses and her mother is saying "Come inside for a cup of tea" while her father gives me a massive welcoming bear hug. Cheryl and her mother scurry off to the kitchen and I am bombarded with questions from the children who speak excellent English.

Later her father takes me on a tour through the vineyard. He trades a few stories about wines and farming and I try my best to appear knowledgeable and intelligent. He is a typical warm-hearted, open and direct Italian and there comes a moment when he gazes at me thoughtfully: "Do you love my daughter?" I look at him sincerely and say: "I love her very much. I would like to share my life with her. I will be kind, caring and faithful to her." Solemnly he extends his hand to shake mine, as if sealing my words into a covenant, and then gives me another huge embrace. Nothing further is said about the matter.

Dinner this evening has something of a celebratory note. The atmosphere is ebullient and joyful. Cheryl's father produces an outstanding Ornellaia and her mother serves memorable culinary delights: crostini di fegato (chicken liver crostini) which is the best I have ever tasted; pasta e fagioli; thick beef steaks which are tender and succulent (rare steaks are the norm in Tuscany and a well done steak is considered a heresy) and fritto misto.

Italians tend to serve many courses, and meals are a relaxing social event, so I am learning to enjoy a conversation over dinner and pace myself. When we finally arrive at the dessert course, I am presented with castagnaccio (chestnut cake) and bongo (chocolate profiteroles). The highlight is amaretto into which we dip cantucci di prato (Tuscan biscotti). Italians sure know how to enjoy their food!

The next day everyone is cleaning and attending to guests, so Cheryl and I take a long walk and return for a swim in the midday sun. I am feeling a bit forlorn as I sense my time with her slipping away. We are laying on our backs on the grass, staring at the sky and talking softly. She is a bit disheartened too. Why can't we have it all? There is always some barrier to happiness in this life: too little money, career struggles, love difficulties, health challenges ...

I am looking into the perfect blue sky and I notice a rumbling black cloud approaching in the distance. And then it's joined by another. And soon the sky fills with pouring rain. Cheryl does not move. I look at her curiously. She smiles and allows the rain to flow over her. I feel a strange sensation as the air goes still around me. Thirty minutes later the sky is a perfect blue again.

Clouds appear. Rain falls. Sky is clear.

I see glimpses of luminous white hair among the olive trees. Could it be?

You have to learn to dance in the rain.

I look at Cheryl. She is hearing it too, and it's a poignant message.

Radical acceptance means Accepting Reality As It Is and then taking responsible Action.

I turn to Cheryl and stroke the wet hair from her face. "I love you, sweetheart." I hold her for a long time. Then she puts her hands on my face and kisses me. She looks at me with intense and vulnerable eyes and then, for the first time ever, she says: "I love you." My heart does a joyful flip-flop.

In the evening we have an exquisite dinner and there is a deep, affectionate rapport around the table. I have been welcomed into this family and now it is up to me to make this work. Acceptance of life as it is and responsible action. I can do this.

The next day is full of goodbyes. In the morning we have a simple breakfast and her mother spills a few tears. I tell her I am deeply appreciative of their kindness and generosity. After effusive hugs we drive home to Florence and spend some time in Cheryl's apartment. We make a commitment to find the way forward. We kiss. We sit closely on the sofa savouring every moment of our time together. We hug each other and there are more tears. A taxi arrives to take me to the airport. Saying goodbye is a blunt knife to the heart.

Cusco, Peru

I am back in London and missing Cheryl like mad. We exchange emails and daily phone calls but there is a hankering in me, a yearning. I want to be with her. I am thinking about all the options and trying to make some decisions.

I am renting a small furnished flat in London so giving notice is the easy part. I need to learn Italian. My career as a therapist will be over if I move to Tuscany. It would be crazy for Cheryl to give up her wonderful home and family. All these thoughts are dashing through my mind and I cannot see the way forward.

The post arrives and I notice a postcard from Peru. I read the big scrawl: *Come to Cusco. It's the final chapter. Jay*

Jay! I can't believe it! How lovely to hear from him. What on earth is he doing in Peru?

I sit down for a moment and consider my finances. I left everything behind in South Africa to start over in London, and this mystical adventure has cost a fortune. But it has been the most incredible journey and I need to find the money to finish it. I am also concerned about Cheryl. How will she feel if I disappear to Peru for a month?

I phone Cheryl and we chat for a while. She is loving and supportive: "I will miss you, but you need to complete your journey. It will be worth it in the end." I phone my father and he sees no sense in what I am doing and says I should focus on earning a living.

November marks the beginning of the rainy season in Peru so I book a flight for early October. It's only one week away, so I rearrange my client schedule and run around collecting everything I need for the trip.

I am in the taxi with my luggage. This is going to be a very tiring journey: check-in at Heathrow airport, early flight to Amsterdam, connecting flight to Lima, arrive six in the evening, overnight stay in Lima, sleep as long as possible, afternoon flight to Cusco the next day. Phew, here we go!

I arrive in Cusco airport (Alejandro Velasco Astete International) and it's a warm twenty-two degrees Celsius. There are plenty of taxis outside and I give the driver the address of my hotel: Andean Wings Boutique Hotel, 225 Siete Cuartones. I remind him that it's very near the Plaza de Armas, the central town square of Cusco. He tells me that it's a popular tourist destination, it's only twenty minutes away and the taxi fare will be less than five dollars.

We arrive and I see a huge door in the wall but there is no sign for the hotel. The taxi driver assures me this is the right place. I walk into the entrance hall and there is a quaint check-in office on the left. The receptionist explains that they have recently opened and are waiting for the outside sign to arrive. Apparently things work a bit slower in Cusco.

Just after the check-in area I enter a large cobbled courtyard surrounded by small pillars and lush plants with a streaming water feature in the centre. The glass ceiling allows an abundance of natural light into a beautiful mauve-and-green dining area. Paintings adorn the walls behind the pillars and there is an offbeat sculpture in the corner. The owner clearly has an artistic eye and pays keen attention to detail.

Most rooms are still unoccupied and I am generously offered a tour of the hotel. Each room is impressively decorated with unique colours and decor, resulting in a distinct personality. The room styles range from bohemian to classic chic with names like Hippie Chic Twin and Inca Presidential Suite. Andean Wings is a truly gorgeous hotel.

My room is the Sacsayhuaman View Mini Suite, so named because from the balcony I can see the White Christ and parts of the Sacsayhuaman complex. The room colour scheme is based on the theories of colour therapy, especially chosen to provide peace and tranquillity. There is also a sumptuous king-size bed and a lovely aromatic bathtub.

The hotel manager suggests a good introduction to the city: one of the daily bus tours of Cusco's sacred archaeological sites, which includes Inca palaces, temples and fortresses. I book a tour for the next morning.

Unlike many Cusco hotels, Andean Wings is just off the central town square. So within minutes I am sitting in the warm sun on the stone steps of the Cathedral of Cusco at the Plaza de Armas. The Church of La Compañia is on my left and an array of restaurants and shops run along the perimeter of the square. The centre of the square is a beautifully manicured park with a large water fountain, old-world street lamps, trees, grass lawns and flower beds. People are relaxing and chatting on the many benches.

This is an interesting place. I am aware of a strange resonance in the air like a spiritual humming. Cusco feels kind of alive.

Welcome to mystical Cusco, one of the most powerful and sacred places on the planet! Jay beams his trademark smile and sits next to me.

"Hey, Jay! It's great to see you!" I give him a brief side-on hug.

The Inca emperors made this city their political, cultural and military capital and ruled over an empire that stretched from modern-day Ecuador through Peru to Bolivia and northern Chile. It has changed a lot over the centuries but you can still feel the sacred power running through the land.

"Yes, I can sense something buzzing under the skin of this place."

Jay sits quietly for a while in the warm sun. I notice how many people turn to look at him as they walk by. He has a somewhat unusual appearance, but there is something more subtle that draws people. Perhaps it has to do with his serene energy.

I am going to Lake Titicaca in a couple of days' time to meet some old friends. Would you like to join me? I nod. Jay always has something up his sleeve and I do not want to miss any of the magic.

The altitude in Cusco is 3,310 metres (10,900 feet) so you may experience mild altitude sickness, ranging from shortness of breath and mild headache to dizziness and nausea. Puno is even higher. So use the next couple of days to acclimatise. Take it very easy and avoid strenuous activity. Drink plenty of bottled still water and Mate de Coca (coca tea) which is available at all hotels and restaurants. This tea is no more stimulating than regular tea but is highly recommended for staving off altitude sickness.

"Yes, doctor." I smile at Jay. I remember the altitude sickness I experienced at Tiger's Nest Monastery in Bhutan. It was not pleasant, so I will take his advice seriously. Jay returns a smile and then, without even a shimmer, he is gone.

The next day I tour the sacred archaeological sites and enjoy the spectacular views of the city and surrounding areas. The tour guide alternates between Latin American Spanish and English and I come away with a clearer understanding of Cusco in the time of the Incas.

The evening is spent relaxing at the Andean Wings hotel. For dinner I enjoy the national dish known as Ceviche (or Cebiche) which is a mixture of raw fish, lime juice, chopped onion and chilli. It is superb. It seems only fitting to accompany this with Peru's well known drink: Pisco Sour, a cocktail of local brandy and lemon juice. After dinner I book a massage for the following evening in the hotel.

The next day I explore the artists' district and numerous craft markets just off the Plaza de Armas. These start just behind the Cathedral of Cusco and continue up a maze of narrow streets. The buildings are really interesting and there is such a range of brightly coloured clothes, souvenirs, traditional dress and paintings that it takes me the better part of the day to view everything.

I return to the hotel with a splendid, vividly coloured oil painting of two hummingbirds collecting nectar. The hummingbird is a sacred symbol of the shamans, as it is the only animal said to have seen the face of God. In the evening I drink more coca tea and enjoy a tasty Lomo Saltado (beef sautéed with onions and peppers) and an equally delicious massage. I sleep deeply and restfully.

In the morning Jay arrives, all snow and cobalt blue in his long white robe. We catch the early morning Andean Explorer train running between Cusco and Puno, which is on the shores of Lake Titicaca. The train has two classes: the Andean Explorer Class and the Backpacker Class. The Andean Explorer Class includes a three-course lunch and access to the glass-walled observation car. Jay produces tickets for the Explorer class and we enjoy ten hours of delightful scenery: magnificent Andean mountains which tower over the deep valleys of the meandering Huatanay River and later the gentle, rolling Andean Plains, speckled with vicuña and alpaca (relatives of the llama).

In the evening I locate the hotel's guest computers and email Cheryl. I want her to know that I am thinking about her and missing her. I receive a lovely email which warms my heart.

Later I hear Jay's voice coming from the restaurant kitchen along with great laughter and merriment. He is no doubt speaking Quechua, the local language, but it's probably his magnetic presence that is converting complete strangers into perfect friends.

Jay appears at my table with our dinner and a bottle of chilled water. *There are no strangers, Steve. On your level of reality everything appears separate but that is part of the grand illusion.*

"You didn't cook that, did you?" I enquire, a bit surprised. He laughs. *Dinner arises from the Source from which everything arises. What do you feel like creating this evening?*

I have no idea what Jay is talking about but I have a hankering for roast lamb and roast potatoes. He lifts the domed cover from my meal … and it's roast lamb and potatoes. I wonder what would happen to the bottle of water if I thought intently about a good Tuscan wine. I sigh gently. I don't know what to believe. I cut into the perfectly cooked lamb and take a bite. It's Karoo lamb and it's delicious. "Thanks for dinner, Jay," I say appreciatively.

The day has been long and when I finally collapse onto my soft bed, it is bliss.

* * *

In the morning a taxi takes us to Puno harbour and we join a group of tourists in a large boat. The guide proudly announces that Lake Titicaca is located on the border of Peru and Bolivia and it sits 3,811 metres (12,500 feet) above sea level, making it the highest commercially navigable lake in the world. Fortunately I am in good shape with no signs of altitude sickness.

Our destination is Uros, just outside Puno, which is a group of over forty artificial islands made from totora, a floating reed that abounds in the shallows of the lake. We arrive and I am completely amazed: every island is nothing more than carefully woven reeds. The islands range from small ones containing just a couple of reed houses and a reed boat to much larger ones resembling small villages. Scattered on the islands are a school, shops, fish farms and numerous crafts stalls designed for the tourists.

Jay disappears for a long while to chat to some of the elders on a private island. When he returns he informs me that their lifestyle and traditions are being challenged by the very tourists who bring much-needed money. It is an interesting dilemma. Jay tells me that this is happening on a much larger scale throughout the world. Capitalism and modern technology are improving the standard of living for many peoples, while simultaneously destroying the very land they live on. Many valuable indigenous medicines and powerful spiritual practices are being lost.

I am beginning to see a wider net being cast by Jay. Perhaps his teachings are not just about meditation and awareness. There is something very pragmatic in his mission, something more than just spiritual techniques. I wonder about Jay. I still know nothing about him. I hear his thought-voice:

If you choose to express yourself in this reality, then you need to deal with issues belonging to this reality. Life in your world is a complex web of political, economic, cultural, ideological and religious strands. These all contribute to the quality and experience of life on your planet.

In the late morning the boat travels on to Taquile, a hilly island about 35 kilometres east of Puno and home to about 3,000 of the Taquile people. Jay wanders off to a council meeting while us tourists are presented with local cuisine, craft stalls and a walk on the island. The Taquile wear traditional black clothes with bright red-striped shawls, and distinctive hats which denote social and relationship status.

We sit on the boat's upper deck on the way back, enjoying the sun and the ocean breeze. I hear Jay once again: *It's hard to see how some people live. Do you know that two percent of your planet's population owns more than half your planet's wealth? And that at least eighty percent of the world's people live on less than ten dollars a day? The rich elite hold the majority of the globe hostage by turning them into debt slaves and so keep the wheel of oppression turning.*

I am stunned into silence. I have never been very political and my mind goes fuzzy when it comes to economics. But something *is* wrong with our world. I see it every day in the newspapers. There are wars across our planet. Vast numbers of people are starving to death. Our planet is being slowly destroyed. What have we let happen to our world?

When we first arrived on this planet we were in awe of its beauty. The air was invigorating and the oceans were clean and pristine. It was an ideal place to support human life. Food was abundant and nutritious and the energy of the planet resonated peace and harmony. Throughout history we sent teachers and scientists to keep you on these paths of vitality and peace. To no avail.

Do you remember Nikola Tesla? One hundred years ago he brought free energy to your planet so the earth would not be ravaged for oil and gas.

He pioneered many revolutionary developments in the field of electromagnetism and registered numerous energy patents. Where is the zero point energy he proposed? What happened to the plans? He died in 1943 and no one remembers him. Look at the condition of your planet now.

Jay looks over at me with a kind, soulful stare: *What will it take for the people of this world to change?* The question lingers in the air, hanging over me like a small electrically charged cloud. Tiny sparks glimmer in my mind but I cannot arrive at an answer.

In the evening I email a passionate message to Cheryl. I love her, I need her, I want to share my life with her! At dinner I imagine for a moment that she is with me, that we are having one of our romantic wine-and-candlelight conversations, that tonight we will fall asleep in each other's arms.

The next morning we catch the Andean Explorer train and begin the long journey back to Cusco. I am staring out the window and thinking a million thoughts: my future with Cheryl in Tuscany; my previous romantic relationships; my life experience over the last few years; my career prospects; and I am speculating about Jay's mission and purpose. My mind feels full and overflowing.

Jay taps my head gently. *That's a lot of birds, Steve. How's your meditation practice going?*

Oh, not this again! Why does it always come back to meditation? "I am sorting through my life, Jay. There's a lot to think about."

Sounds important. Do you have a clear intention? Have you painted the dream?

"What do you mean?"

Thinking is not going to solve the problem. You're just going round in circles and getting frustrated and anxious. What is your clear intention?

"I want to be with Cheryl. Preferably in beautiful Tuscany."

Jay places his hand on mine and instantly everything turns into light. *Show me. Paint your dream onto this blank canvas.*

All around me is pure whiteness. Nothing but white. I have no idea what to do. I feel a bit apprehensive and a small black cloud appears in the distance. Oops, that was probably me. The cloud gets bigger and moves toward us. How annoying! A light red tinges the whiteness and lightning flashes. I can master this! A flock of birds flits across the canvas scattering colours everywhere. This isn't going too well.

Jay is intently watching my paltry efforts. *Looks like hard work.*

I wave my hands to distract the birds from their chaotic mission. Shoo! I feel even more frustrated and suddenly we are surrounded by red rivulets. Oh no! More clouds arrive and soon Jay and I are standing in driving rain and thunder. Jay pulls a chair out of nowhere and sits down. Why is he smiling? I am drenched and despondent.

I stop for a moment and look around. Jay offers me a chair. There is a slight break in the weather. Oh. Maybe the weather is caused by my emotions. Maybe this weather *is* my emotions. I am really tired, so I give up trying and just watch the messy picture until things start to settle. Birds are still flying everywhere.

Jay is sitting next to me and he begins to blur. The scene is shifting back to clear whiteness. There are a few birds but I am no longer attaching to them. If they appear, I just observe them. I notice that

Jay is disappearing and I feel a moment of panic. A few birds streak overhead. I witness my feelings and the birds gradually vanish.

How is this happening? I am not *doing* anything. Instantly more birds appear. I let go and surrender again. I am just being. And here, alone in the nothingness, I blink. There is nothing here but my thoughts and my emotions. I am just watching and witnessing. I am *being!* A sudden feeling of delight comes over me and a glorious sunrise appears on my canvas. Wow, am I creating all this?

In the far distance walks a Bhutanese monk and I hear: *It is not about doing, rather about being. When you do, you cannot be. When you be, you can do anything.*

And for the first time, I truly get it. Something switches on. I am in the Now. There is nothing but this precious Moment. My chair falls over and dissolves. Everything is pure soft whiteness. I am with Cheryl in Florence. I am standing in the front room of her apartment. She looks at me with that gorgeous smile and my heart skips a beat.

There is a bottle of champagne on the glass coffee table. I walk over and fill the two glasses. There is a yellow note on the table: *Remember to allow the flow of Life.* I have no idea what this means but I surrender to the notion. Within moments a powerful flow of divine light pours through me and into Cheryl's apartment, lighting everything in diffuse gold and bathing us in soft ethereal music.

I look into Cheryl's eyes and raise my glass: "To our love." She clinks my glass and slips her arm around my waist and we gaze at the splendid cherry-red Tuscan sunset.

When I return to the Andean Explorer reality, I find that I am alone in the carriage. I feel remarkably calm and peaceful. I am no longer chased by confusing thoughts and emotions. I look at the time and hours have passed. We will arrive in Cusco soon and I would like to enjoy the panoramic landscape before it recedes from view.

I walk to the glass-walled observation car and see a throng of people surrounding a familiar white-haired figure. What is he up to now? I move in closer and hear Jay's voice resonating so clearly that it feels as if he is standing right next to me.

"There was once a king who had an opulent palace set among vast farmlands. Numerous servants cared for him and he lived a peaceful existence surrounded by everything his heart could possibly desire. In this most serene world he became afflicted by boredom and began to question if he was truly alive. One day the king, dressed only in servant's clothes, took a walk through the forest just outside the palace. The king seldom walked alone. Soon a heavy branch fell from high above and landed on his head, concealing all his memory.

"When the king regained consciousness, he assumed that he must be a lowly peasant. He did not know who he was and did not seem to have any working skills, so he was reviled by his fellow peasants. The king had no choice but to become a beggar. Over the next few years this beggar tried desperately to understand who he was and why he never seemed to belong anywhere.

"One day a young girl from the palace recognised him. She said to him that it was not necessary to beg, that he was in fact a king. The beggar stared at her in disbelief and finally he burst into laughter. He patted her head and sent her on her way. The little girl turned and looked back just once. Sadness filled her eyes and she wondered what it would take for the king to awaken."

The people surrounding Jay are mesmerised and mystified. The carriage feels charged with a serene and powerful energy. An arrival announcement causes everyone to suddenly disperse.

The words I speak are just seeds, Steve. They may only sprout in a few weeks' or even a few years' time. Each person understands the story on some level. But it's not about the story. It's about the transmission of enlightened energy so the soil becomes fertile and the seeds can grow.

I look at him and nod. For once I understand what he is saying. I wonder why he is telling me this. "Jay –" The train lurches and we hasten to collect our daypacks from the carriage before disembarking.

It is much later and I am ruminating alone at the wonderful Andean Wings over a leisurely and delicious dinner. I had a breakthrough today and at last I have an increased understanding of Jay's cryptic teachings. There are still many questions but for now I feel content.

Later in the evening I receive an email from Cheryl in which she describes a brilliant daydream about us drinking champagne and watching the Tuscan sunset together. I have to smile. What is this mystical world I have entered?

* * *

In the morning Jay arrives early and has breakfast with me. *I thought today would be a great time to visit the Sacred Valley and Machu Picchu. Everything has been arranged. Interested?*

I look up enthusiastically. "Yes!" Everyone has heard of mysterious Machu Picchu. Jay pushes a pamphlet across the table. *See you outside in half an hour. And remember your hat and sunglasses.*

Machu Picchu (Old Mountain) is a pre-Columbian 15th-century Inca site. The altitude at the Gateway of the Sun, the highest point you are likely to reach, is 2,500 metres (8,200 feet) so it is lower in altitude than Cusco. Machu Picchu is situated on a mountain ridge above the Urubamba Valley approximately 80 kilometres (50 miles) northwest of Cusco. It is often referred to as The Lost City of the Incas, as the site was never discovered by the Spanish during their conquest.

There is a direct train line between Cusco and Machu Picchu but Jay has decided to drive via the towns of Pisac and Ollantaytambo. The journey to Pisac takes about 45 minutes and when we arrive we spend an hour walking through the huge open-air market and craft stalls. It takes another hour and a half to drive from Pisac to Ollantaytambo and the views of the Sacred Valley along the route are lush and spectacular.

At Ollantaytambo we park the car and spend some time walking through the Ollantaytambo ruins and fortress. After a light lunch we finally catch the afternoon train to Machu Picchu. The scenic train journey runs along the Urubamba river, briefly intersecting with the Inca Trail (which is the only other way to reach Machu Picchu).

The town of Machu Picchu has been named after the mountain and it is very much a tourist town packed with hotels, shops and restaurants. After a brief walk around, we check in and refresh ourselves with tea and cake in the hotel lounge. I am experiencing some excitement mixed with a vague sense of unease and I have no idea why I am feeling this way. After dinner I stare at the television for a while and then have an early night.

The next morning Jay is cheerful and full of energy. I still feel strangely apprehensive. We catch the bus and it zigzags along curved dirt roads for about half an hour to reach the mountain. At the entrance we show our tickets and I am offered a Machu Picchu stamp for my passport which I happily accept.

We spend the entire morning walking along the glorious mountain top with Jay explaining the various temples, palaces, shrines, dwellings, plazas, streets and paths. He seems to know this place extremely well and for a brief moment I notice a look of wistful longing. This place must have been awe-inspiring in its day.

When we reach one of the highest viewing points I see the entire breathtaking expanse of buildings, stone ruins, grass steps and magnificent mountain heads. We rest here and enjoy our sandwiches and water. After a while Jay gives me a serious look. *I would like to take you on a journey after lunch. It may be a few hours and will be the most difficult journey you have ever experienced. I can't tell you more. It is up to you.*

Is this why I have felt so uneasy? I think for a few moments. "Jay, I trust you. I have come this far and am finally starting to understand your teachings. I'll do it." I swallow hard. What have I let myself in for?

After lunch we walk to the Temple of the Sun. In the lower part of the temple lies a royal tomb, which has a strange diagonal-shaped entrance with steps carved into the rock on one side. Jay leads us inside the tomb, places his hands against the solid back wall and begins uttering other-worldly sounds. A doorway opens and Jay ushers me into a secret chamber. The chamber is big enough to stand comfortably and stretch out in all directions. The temperature is warm and there is a fresh breeze coming from somewhere. Jay gives me a hug and looks kindly at me. *I will come and get you when you're done.*

I bite my lip and watch Jay close the strange doorway. It is now pitch black in here. I feel a moment of panic and rush to the doorway but feel only solid rock. I am trapped! I shout Jay's name a few times. A million birds rush into my sky. I can't escape! I will die here! I need to get out! I am scared and light-headed and my heart is racing.

In the midst of raw fear I hear a little Tuscan angel saying "Radical acceptance, my love." I burst into tears. I will never see Cheryl again! What am I doing here? What if Jay doesn't come back? I don't know anything about Jay! I slump to the hard floor in despair. What use are all the lessons Jay has taught me? I cannot escape this situation.

I take a few long, deep breaths and try to calm down and gather my thoughts. There is nothing I can do except watch and witness my own mind. Is this the reason Jay has placed me in this chamber? Perhaps I need to master the meditation practice.

I cast my mind back to the teachings. Meditation is not supposed to be hard work; if I intensely watch the birds then I lose the point of meditation. It is not about striving and doing, it is about Surrender. It is not about running away, it is about Letting Go. It is not about struggle, it is about Being.

I allow myself to simply *be* in the tomb, accepting what is, staying in the Moment. I watch the birds flit across my sky. I do not attach to them and they come and go as they please. Eventually most of the birds dissipate and my emotions subside.

Time seems to stand still in here. Who told me that the past is only a dream and the future is only an idea? And that everything is Now?

I notice my thoughts are slowing and there are gaps with no thought. If I am *witnessing* my mind and my senses, then I am not my mind nor my senses. Who is doing the witnessing? Who is *being*? Who am I?

I exist. All I know is: I AM CONSCIOUS AND I EXIST. I find myself existing.

What is the meaning of my life? Higher and more powerful beings like parents, society, culture and media have imposed meaning onto my life, but that is not actual meaning. The *meaning of my life is not defined by people and events outside of me*. How can *external* things decide a meaning for me?

I was born into a particular physical body with its distinct qualities and appearance. But I am not my body and *my body cannot give me meaning*. I have a mind with unique abilities and varying degrees of emotional, logical, intellectual, kinaesthetic, artistic, musical and spatial intelligence, just like every other human being, but I am not my mind and *my mind cannot give me meaning*.

I have dispositions, talents and interests which drive me and encourage me to lead a certain lifestyle but *none of these give me meaning*.

All I know is: I AM CONSCIOUS AND I EXIST. I find myself existing. All meaning is imposed from the outside. There is no intrinsic or innate meaning. I have no inbuilt meaning.

I know life exists because I am alive. I know consciousness exists because I am conscious. Life just is. Consciousness just is. Life and consciousness have no intrinsic or inbuilt meaning.

I have no meaning. I just am. Life has no meaning. Life just is.

It feels like hours are passing in this dark chamber. As I journey to the extreme of who I am, I realise that I am alone. *I have always felt alone.* I have sought love, romance, sex, social connection, friendship and belonging just to appease this aloneness. And while these have felt good, I always feel alone inside. Nothing from the *outside* can fill up this aloneness. How can something that is outside of me, something that is *separate* and *external* to me, fill up my aloneness?

On an unconscious level I have always known that I am alone and without meaning. This has made me feel a deep emptiness in my core. And this emptiness has created all the difficulties and drama and pain in my life. Every dream I have pursued and every person I have chased has been for one reason: to fill this deep emptiness in me.

I AM ALONE AND WITHOUT MEANING.

There is nothing special about me. Nothing I attain or achieve will ever validate me or give me meaning. No one I love, and no one I share my life with, will ever take away this aloneness. No amount of friendship, status, rewards, fame or wealth will ever fill this emptiness deep inside me.

I AM ALONE AND WITHOUT MEANING.

I am crying in the dark. Tears are streaming down my face. I am shouting "Why? Why?" There is a fierce sadness in my heart. Waves of nausea grip me. I quickly slip into the deepest and most intense emotional pain I have ever felt. For what seems like ages, I am rendered completely thoughtless and wordless and slowly drown in existential agony.

There is no further or deeper or lower I can go. This is the end of the road. This is what has preyed in the back of my mind all my life. Stalking me, scaring me in my quiet moments. I have unknowingly fought against this creeping monster or run away from it for as long as I can remember. But it is *in* me. It is part of me and there is no escape.

I cannot go on anymore. I cannot continue in this way. I give up. I surrender. I SURRENDER!

In this agonising moment, in this utter despair, I start to feel a flicker of light. At this bleak rock-bottom something wondrous is happening: a wave of pleasure. Now a rush of ecstasy. And now a slow explosion of bliss from my deepest core. Nothing I have ever experienced can describe this. I cannot speak. I can barely move. I am enveloped and overwhelmed from the inside out by a rapturous euphoria.

It is much later and I hear the rock doorway opening. There stands Jay, all smiling and admiring. *Well done, Steve.* He helps me to my feet and I stagger out into the light. I squint and Jay tells me it is late afternoon.

We sit outside for a while and I notice how incredibly green the mountain vegetation appears; the grass seems to dance in front of me; a lone tree shimmers brilliantly; and the clouds seem to be playing a sonata in the luminous sky.

It's a leisurely stroll back to the bus and I have no desire to say a word. I feel tender and vulnerable. Jay keeps a watchful eye on me. After an undisturbed bus ride and a quiet dinner, I fall into bed and sleep for what feels like a month.

The next day we catch the late morning train to Cusco. I am reflectively integrating my experience and quietly enjoying the beautiful scenery. Jay appears to be absorbed in a book. I glance at the cover: The Shock Doctrine by Naomi Klein. Never heard of it. *You should read this sometime, Steve. It's a real eye-opener. It's an education about your world.*

When we arrive in Cusco, Jay gives me a gentle hug. *Take it easy for the rest of the day. See you day after tomorrow.* And I do just that. I keep mostly to myself, perusing the craft markets, artists' shops and cathedrals and enjoying some time in the spa. I eat healthily and drink lots of water. On both nights I fall into a deep and dreamless slumber.

* * *

Jay arrives and seats himself at the breakfast table. "Good morning, Steve. How are you?"

"Morning, Jay. Good thanks ... although it feels like I've lost a few layers. I know what I experienced but my mind has not caught up yet. There's a lot to process."

Well, the good news is that we are going to the Temple of the Moon this morning. It is one of the most sacred and powerful places on the planet and one of our best-kept secrets. I think you will enjoy it.

I am still feeling a little tender but I am keen to see more of amazing Cusco. So I finish my breakfast and grab a daypack and we're off.

We spend the morning walking through the endless hills, looking at interesting rock outcrops, strange carvings and sacred stones.

The Cusco hum that usually buzzes in the background seems stronger in this place. I have never felt such a charged atmosphere anywhere.

I want to ask Jay about this but we suddenly stop in front of a peculiar square indent on a rock wall. Jay touches the small square with his hand and once again a doorway appears in the solid rock. He smiles encouragingly. *Come on, it's perfectly safe. I will stay with you the whole time.*

The doorway closes behind us and reverts to solid rock. A strange bluish light illuminates the steps which lead down a narrow passageway. I notice that the hum is more intense. I wonder where on earth we are going.

The passageway begins to widen and the light becomes bluish-white. After about fifteen minutes we come to an enormous cavern, and in the centre of the cavern is a softly pulsating three-dimensional mist that looks like a midnight star-filled sky. It's the most beautiful and profound thing I have ever seen.

"What is it, Jay?"

It is a vehicle for journeying through different dimensions. It travels anywhere you can imagine.

"You mean like other planets and other civilisations?"

It depends where you are in your evolution. If you still choose to use your physical body then this vehicle can be used to travel to other planets, provided you stay in physical worlds.

"What do you mean? Are there worlds that are not physical?"

Jay is smiling. *Everything exists as a possibility. There are many dimensions. You are focusing your consciousness in just one or two.*

"I don't understand. Are there layers of reality around me that I cannot perceive with these limited physical senses?"

A dimension isn't a layer, it is an expression of Life. And you are not your body or your mind, remember? You are consciousness, and your consciousness is like a torch shining in a particular direction, lighting up only one dimension.

"Jay, that is deep." I raise my elbows high while rubbing my eyes with the back of my hands. I yawn and stretch like a cat. I am feeling tired and a bit spaced out.

Different dimensions are expressions of Life. As you shift your consciousness, you can step into these other dimensions. It is just a matter of shining your torch in another direction.

I look at him quizzically.

Step inside and I'll show you. You have progressed sufficiently to be able to do this.

We walk into the blue starry mist. It feels strangely alive and deeply serene at the same time. He gives me a quick warning: *Hold on tight, Steve!* And then the air is crackling and I am moving in a vortex of rapid geometric blues, reds, yellows and greens. Am I moving or is the vortex moving? It is intense and powerful. My body begins shaking and my mind is soon overwhelmed.

I wake up. Jay is gently touching my shoulder. *Hey, Steve. The first two or three times will often floor a consciousness that is used to only one dimension. Shall we try again?*

It is the fifth time in the stunning vortex of colours. I know what to expect now and I realise that my body has nothing to do with this. I am travelling somewhere vastly different to my old physical reality. I hold my intention strongly; I am determined to stay conscious this time. I see an extremely bright light at the end of the swirling tunnel and I focus on this as my destination.

A doorway opens on my left and I am sucked into a world of liquid green tranquillity. A number of nebulous beings surround me and the energy feels curious. *What is it doing here? It does not belong here.* Odd bubbles of light float past. I hear perplexing sounds – is it music? *It is a young energy far from home.* There is a flash and I find myself standing outside the mist in the cavern.

"That was amazing! What happened? Where was I?"

Those beings are ancient ambassadors of peace. They have mastered the expression of utter tranquillity and don't interact anymore.

"Can I have another go?"

Step inside and set your intention. You're controlling this.

Once I get the hang of it, I am flying across wild and bright geometry and experiencing one mind-boggling expression after another. Each doorway is a portal into unseen colours, unheard sounds and fantastical expressions of life. The beings I meet are intelligent, kind, inquisitive, spiritual, fun, strange, bizarre, absurd and extraordinary. Some of them impart brief words of wisdom: *Spread peace in your world ... Love is All.*

I am now able to ride this vortex with relative ease. It goes on forever with myriads of doorways appearing and receding. Sometimes I can choose to enter a doorway, sometimes it chooses me. This may be a two-way street. The bright light seems to stay at the end of the tunnel and just once I manage to get near it, and

I hear an authoritative voice thunder *YOU ARE NOT WELCOME HERE!* I am instantly thrown out of the vortex and find myself back in the cavern.

"That was something, Jay. What is the Light that rejected me?"

That is exactly the point. You will understand in time.

I suddenly feel sick and I am sweating profusely. I try to stand but my legs are unsteady, then I lean forward and throw up. I feel terrible.

Jay grabs my hand and shimmers. I find myself lying on my bed at the Andean Wings. For two days I have a fever and my body runs hot and cold with shivers. I ache and my limbs feel heavy. I sleep most of the time and float through dozens of worlds, unsure what is a dream and what is reality.

* * *

On the third day I return to full health. In the morning I phone Cheryl. I need to hear her voice. It's early evening in Florence and she sounds tired when she answers. We both light up immediately: "I miss you!" she says. "I love you!" I respond. We chat for about twenty minutes both wanting to hear more news. It is so lovely to talk with her and it's so hard to say goodbye.

Jay comes over to see how I am. He is smiling and has a knowing look in his eye. We take a stroll to the Plaza de Armas and sit on a park bench. *How's your body feeling? How are you doing?*

"My body feels a bit strange … like I don't belong in it. Have I become part of every reality I have visited? I am not sure where my home is now."

It takes time to adjust to having your consciousness in multiple dimensions. You now have a number of residences across All That Is.

I feel more relaxed when he explains this. I look around and notice that everything is liquid green. "Very amusing, Jay."

It is not me who is doing this, Steve. Do you feel like coming back to the Plaza de Armas now?

In a flash I am back on the park bench. I stand up shocked: "What the – how – ?"

You are going to have to work on your control a bit more. Jay laughs and then proceeds to jump us to sixteen different worlds without so much as blinking an eye. *See? It's not so difficult.*

I gasp and stumble back to this reality. "This is messing with my head."

This has nothing to do with your mind or your body. You are consciousness and your intention directs your journey. Your limited mind only gets in the way.

I am staring directly ahead, rapidly blinking. "So if I put my mind aside and move into *being* and set my intention …" I move through five new worlds in quick succession. "What the - ?"

Bingo! I think he's got it.

I begin to feel nauseous again. I need to take it easy and let my body catch up. Or is it my mind? Or is that a limiting belief *from* my mind? A shock of knowing fills me: THE ONLY LIMITS ARE IN MY MIND. I am free! I am FREE!

I bounce around a dozen worlds and back to the park bench and then do another five just for good measure. I feel exhilarated. I feel healthy. I feel fantastic.

Back in this reality I see Jay watching me thoughtfully. He stands up. *I have some things to do. Enjoy the rest of this day. Tomorrow we are going to see the Q'ero.*

I am alone on a park bench in a strange world. This used to be my world; now there are many places where I reside. My mind is my only limitation and I don't believe it anymore. This body-mind is only an expression of *this* reality and has nothing to do with the real me. I am consciousness and I can be expressed in any reality. I have to smile. It's mind-blowing!

I sit for a while in the cooling air. Huge rain clouds have filled the sky and it begins to pour. I run to shelter under the covered walkway near the shops. Framed by the archway, I watch the rainstorm drench the park and the imposing Church of La Compañia across the square.

I spend the rest of the afternoon with a good book, hot chocolate and cake. That's enough travelling for one day.

* * *

"Today you are going to meet the grandchildren of the Inca." Jay breezes into breakfast in his usual jovial manner. "They call themselves the Q'ero and they are the humblest beings of light you will ever meet. This will be the final stage of your long journey."

"Awesome!" I raise my arms jubilantly. "Who exactly are the Q'ero?"

They are an indigenous people who have kept themselves hidden from the world by living at great altitudes in the Andes mountains, as high as 16,000 feet. They have preserved the ancient spiritual practices and we call them Keepers of the Ancient Knowledge. They are now choosing to reveal themselves in order to bring guidance to humankind. This is happening because your world has approached a critical turning point.

I grab my backpack and sunglasses and jump in the car, and we drive to meet the horses. Then the arduous journey to meet the Q'ero begins. I enjoy horse riding but this is not very comfortable and my breathing is a bit laboured. I wonder why we don't just shimmer to meet the Q'ero.

You are about to enter a magical kingdom. Do not be fooled by appearances. These are poor weavers, corn and potato farmers and alpaca and llama herders. Life is very hard up here. However, the Q'ero are the masters of the living energy. They show us how we are meant to live on this planet.

Everything looks pretty ordinary but as we ascend I notice a different world. There is something quite subtle, something just beyond the ordinary senses. "Jay, are we entering another expression of reality? No wait … are we going further down the tunnel of light?"

Jay turns and looks at me. His eyes are twinkling as he smiles. *Sometimes I don't think you need a teacher at all.*

The long trip encourages me into a contemplative mood. There seems to be an important piece of the puzzle still missing. It's like discovering the answer on the tip of your tongue, just out of reach.

We pass a few Q'ero and Jay stops for a brief chat. The discussion seems quite animated and the Q'ero look at me as if they know something. I hear a low-level ringing in my ears and feel a bit light-headed. Perhaps it's the onset of altitude sickness. One of the Q'ero stretches out his hand and within moments a hummingbird appears and hovers intently around me. I am not sure what is happening, so I smile and nod my head in gratitude. Soon we are on our way again.

Do you know that the Q'ero believe that everything is consciousness and everything is energy? They converse as easily with mountains and trees and birds as they do with their fellow human beings.

Why is Jay telling me this? Why do I feel so weird? I think my mind is tripping on the magnitude of it all. What if every reality is no more than a doorway in that swirling colourful vortex? What if every reality is just a playground? What if every reality is just Life dancing? Should we take any of it seriously?

We finally arrive at Chua Chua, a village located at a dizzying 14,500 feet. There are twelve Q'ero waiting for us, dressed in warm ponchos and brightly coloured hats. They look so simple and ordinary but I remember Jay's cautionary words.

Soon I am introduced to a world of visionaries, dreamers, diviners, healers and spirit travellers. Each Q'ero carries a mesa (a fabric bundle holding their most sacred objects) and is an expert in a particular area of shamanism. They are all masters of the living energy.

The Q'ero masters, like many masters, only show you what you are ready to understand. This may result in some people not realising that they are actually in the presence of a master. Others get frustrated by the apparent slowness of the teaching or the lack of information. Remember, it is not the words that teach. It's the transmission of enlightened energy.

Over the next few days the Q'ero take turns in sharing their simple and profound knowledge. I learn to taste energy, experiment with filaments of light and move the life force in plants, animals, trees and mountains. I enjoy wordless mystical communication with the stars at night and the sun during the day. I play with intention, dreams and visions and together we plant despachos to change and create realities. We surf the waves of cosmic energy and travel to different worlds together.

I learn about an ancient philosophy based on energy, compassion, freedom, unconditional love and radical respect for all living beings. I sense their deep connection to the planet, their concern about the future of humankind and the pressing need to bring about positive change. I begin to understand their childlike curiosity, their amazing ability to completely live in the moment and their deep appreciation of the mystery of life.

After a week, I am sitting with Jay overlooking the beautiful mountainside. "Jay, this is not the pinnacle of it all, is it? There are many quiet masters around our world. There are masters on other worlds. Is this a doorway that is very close to the Light?"

Jay smiles at me. *Get some sleep tonight and we will start your final journey in the morning. It will be right here in the open air.*

In my dreams I am in a hotel with a hundred floors and ten thousand doors and I am searching in slow motion. There are very bright windows at the end of each corridor and the air is syrupy and it's difficult to move and I need to find the key ... where is it? ... where is it?

* * *

In the morning we walk to a rocky sheltered enclave. The sun is shining brightly and the air feels crisp and fresh. We are alone. I am excited and apprehensive.

Do you remember your first and most important lesson?

"Um, the seagulls on the beach in South Africa? That huge circle in the air?"

Jay waves his hand and a huge circle of seagulls is squawking in the Peruvian sky. "Those surely can't be seagulls, Jay."

Why not? Are you limiting my reality? Pay close attention. Those seagulls have formed together in a special way. Is there anything in the circle?

"No. It's just sky. The same bright blue sky that is on the outside of the circle. Everything is sky but those birds have created a circle."

And what are those birds?

"The birds are my thoughts: beliefs, values, stories, ideology and ideas pushed into me from parents, society, culture and the media. All just thoughts. And emotions ... but emotions are thoughts on fire. So it's all just thoughts in my mind."

Jay's eyes are supportive and flowing compassion. *Tell me what you see. Is there anything but the sky and the gulls?*

"There is only sky and gulls."

What about the circle that the gulls appear to have formed? Does the circle have an identity or a personality of its own? Does it actually exist on its own, independently of the gulls?

"No, of course not. There is only sky and the illusion of a circle formed by the gulls. As soon as the gulls fly away that circle will simply disappear."

That circle appears real when there are so many birds. Jay pauses and looks intently at me. *Who are you when all your thoughts have flown away?*

That weird sensation has started again. Time is slowing down. As I watch the circle of birds, they start to spread out and form a tunnel. Now I can see bright blue sky at the end of the tunnel.

Who are you without your thoughts and stories? What happens when you let go of all those birds? When you surrender?

"There is nothing, Jay!" I shout. "When the birds are gone there is only sky. When I was trapped in the tomb I lost all my birds and I was excruciatingly EMPTY. That emptiness has caused all the drama, pain and anguish in my life."

Yes ... there is emptiness inside you. Beyond your thoughts and stories there is nothing.

He leans over and touches me on the forehead. There is a whizzing sensation and suddenly I am in the vortex flying through the wild, pulsating colours. All the doors are firmly closed and I am propelled to the Light at the end of the tunnel. The vortex slowly disintegrates, and a voice of great authority says:

YOU ARE NOT WELCOME HERE!

I am floating in limbo. It's hard to think. What did Evan say about the waves in the sea? Or was that Cheryl? What if there are no birds in the sky? The idea of the dance and the playground ... that agonising experience in the tomb ...

YOU ARE NOT WELCOME HERE!

I am not my thoughts ... I am stuck here ... all these realities ... I asked for this ... I am not my mind ... I am not my body ... Who am I? ... oh ... my ... there is bright blue light everywhere ... I need that last answer ...

YOU ARE NOT WELCOME HERE!

Oh!

I do not exist. It is the 'I' that is not welcome here! The illusory circle caused by my thoughts is 'I', but it is not real. I do not exist! When the birds are gone, my true nature is exposed. It is beyond emptiness or lack of me.

When the birds are gone, there is only Sky. When the thoughts disappear, there is only Life. When the doors are ignored, there is only Light.

"I DO NOT EXIST!"

Instantly I am pulled into the Light. For what seems like ages, I am swimming in rivers of ecstasy and bliss ... beyond words, beyond incredible ... then there is ... nothing ... at all. Nothing. There is nothing to see, nothing to experience and nothing to do. But this is *not* emptiness or nothing. I am floating in something. I am drowning in the Source of it All.

I can't find myself. I don't exist. Oh ... my ... I AM NOTHING BUT CONSCIOUSNESS SWIMMING IN CONSCIOUSNESS. Beyond all the birds, all the forms, and all the illusions of the infinite realities, there is nothing but pure unmanifested Consciousness. Nothing but Consciousness.

I am consciousness swimming in Consciousness. There is nothing but Consciousness. There is nothing but One Consciousness. I am this One Consciousness! I am Life!

I am not alone or separate after all. How can I be? I do not exist separately to this Consciousness. I am this Consciousness. I am Pure Awareness. I am Life.

There is nothing but One Consciousness. I am Light. I am Life. I am the Creator of All. I look down a million tunnels at a zillion doors which are no more than my Thoughts. There is only Pure Awareness which manifests Thoughts that create the illusion of different realities.

Everything that is manifest, every reality that exists, is a Thought created by Me. I am Consciousness. All consciousness is Me. I am the Pure Awareness that manifests everything. Every reality, every human being, every mountain, every bird, every tree – is nothing but a manifestation of Consciousness. Everything *is*

Consciousness. Everything has as its true nature only Me. I am Consciousness. I am God.

I am Consciousness ... I am Life ... I am Light ... I am Pure Awareness ... I am God ...

"I AM!"

I notice the body-mind in Stephen's reality jumps up and shouts. He is sitting high up in the Andes mountains next to a being of light called Jay. I am the One Consciousness manifesting Steve and Jay and the mountain. They are just my Thoughts. There is nothing but Me.

"I AM!"

A fragment of my Consciousness became so entrenched in the reality of Stephen that it forgot Itself. It was swallowed in the illusion of that Thought. Stephen was just a film that I created. Now I remember that I am the Watcher, I am the Creator. That fragment of my Consciousness called Stephen has awakened. It remembers who It is.

"I AM!"

All these Thoughts – Jay, Stephen, Cheryl, Evan, the Q'ero, the mountains, the beaches, the sky, the birds – are simply manifestations of Me. All is One. Everything is One Consciousness.

"I Am."

I am God. I am all that Is. I am the Source of All. I am Is-ness, Source, Pure Consciousness, Pure Awareness, Light and Life. I am the existence of every possibility.

"I Am."

Life has no meaning. Life just Is. All Life is pure potential, a sea of possibilities, manifesting in an unlimited myriad of ways, forms and realities. This is the great Dance of Life.

"I Am."

What then of Love? There is only One Consciousness, One Being. Love is when the manifested illusions meet and awaken. Love is Life meeting Itself. Love is the acceptance of every possibility. Love is the dissolution of the illusory self and the return to the Light. Love is the Awakening. Love is coming Home.

I hear Jay's voice in the background: *That's brilliant, Steve. But what of all the sadness, greed and pain in this world?*

"When Consciousness is lost and believes that it exists separately, then it will always experience the illusion of agonising emptiness and separateness. This pain is usually hidden on a very deep level and manifests as loneliness, fear, anxiety, depression, duality, greed and aggression."

Where to from here?

"The only way forward for this planet, indeed for any reality, is for every being to awaken. For God in every dimension to remember Itself."

Welcome Home, Steve.

Jay goes for a walk to meet with the Q'ero. He leaves me alone for hours. In the hard dirt I see he has scrawled these words: 'Form is emptiness. Emptiness is form. All is One.' I just smile. I have no need to move and no desire to do anything. I am Here. I am Now. I am Life. I am Light. I am Pure Awareness. I am the One Consciousness.

"I Am."

* * *

How strange to return to this body-mind. To be in this reality once again. To come to the end of this wild and wonderful spiritual journey.

I know now that everything I have ever experienced – pain, pleasure, sadness, triumph, disaster, tragedy, joy, trauma – has pushed me toward this one point: Enlightenment. To fall into the Light. To drown in the Light. To realise the illusion of the self and find ultimate freedom in the Light.

Discovering one's true nature and returning to Source is the destination of every living being. All roads lead to Awakening. Every path intends that Consciousness will wake up and remember Who It really Is.

I Am.

Saying goodbye is hard. A celebration dinner with the Q'ero. A couple of nights at the Andean Wings. Big hugs and Jay's final words: *One journey is complete. The other is just beginning. The rest of the journey is up to you.*

London, England

It is late November and the weather in England is cooling considerably. The mornings are becoming bitter. It's time to get out the warm coat, scarf and gloves.

I am sitting in my therapist's chair contemplating my life: How is it that I have found spectacular bliss and completeness, discovered my true nature and awakened ... and yet I feel so lost? Everything I knew and understood has changed. My old life has disintegrated. I have shifted fundamentally and I have no idea what I am doing in this world. Aren't enlightened beings supposed to have all the answers?

The phone in my office rings. It's my father: he has been diagnosed with lung cancer. I listen in stupefied silence. I go over and see him immediately. He looks at me with his usual resolute stare and shows little emotion. I offer him any support he needs.

I talk to Cheryl in the evening. It is good to hear her voice. I pour out my mixed thoughts and emotions: Why am I in tears when my father is stoical? What has happened to my life? Has everything descended into chaos? How can we live together? How can I leave England with my father in this condition? Enlightenment has left me with nothing to teach, nothing to attain and nothing to do! Cheryl calmly listens and makes soothing noises. She makes plans to visit me in a couple of weeks' time and stay through Christmas.

The next few months are a blur of visiting my father in hospital and watching his body slowly deteriorate. A lung operation does not improve his condition and the cancer spreads through his body. He never cries, never shows fear, never says how he is feeling. It seems that impending death will not change his controlled exterior. The morphine drip means that he sleeps a lot and he shares some of his peculiar dreams with me.

In the middle of February, the palliative manager at the hospital sits me down and says: "It's the last days of his life." They move my father to a hospice. I try not to cry in front of my dad. He holds my hand briefly and says he loves me. Tears stream down my face.

It is April 8th. This morning my father married a wonderful woman (his long-term partner) and now it's 11pm and they have just phoned to say he has moved to the next world. My chest aches and I cry deeply.

It is late May. It is my birthday. My father appears in my dreams. We are in a sunny garden and birds are twittering around a fountain. I am sad and I find myself crying. He sits watching me for a while and then in typical fashion says: "What do you want to do with your life? Make it count!"

It is June and I am sitting on the leather sofa with Cheryl in her beautiful home in Florence. She looks concerned, and in her usual gentle way she asks: "Has your father's passing changed your thoughts about your life? Has your awakening experience changed your feelings toward me?" I grab her hand and look deeply into her eyes. "Cheryl, I do feel different but I still love you with all my heart … and I want to spend the rest of my life with you."

She jumps on me and giggles excitedly. "Move in with me! I don't care if you can't work as a therapist. I don't care if you have little money. There is plenty of room in my house. Love is worth being brave for and risking everything."

It is July and I am sitting in Avebury, near Marlborough, in England. I am surrounded by the sacred stones. A fresh breeze is blowing. The weather is warm and the sun is beaming brightly onto the grass. There are a few sheep grazing across the way. I am lost in a million thoughts when I hear Jay's whisper: *Do you have a clear intention? Have you painted the dream?*

"Jay!" I burst into smiles and give him a big hug. "What are you doing here?" His metallic blue eyes flash kindly. *I should be asking you that question, Steve.*

I shrug my shoulders and sigh deeply. "I am lost, Jay. There is nothing to learn, nothing to teach, nothing to do, nothing to achieve, nothing to attain. I am Light and Life and Bliss. I Am. I don't know what I am doing in this reality anymore."

From where I am sitting, you have a few choices: You exit this reality and stay in the Light; you surf through different realities enjoying the great Dance of Life; or you stay in this reality and make a difference on this planet. These are the choices for every enlightened being.

"Is this what you meant by the second journey?"

Yes. Every experience you have ever had, and every moment of every lifetime, has been leading you toward enlightenment. Every being is treading the same path, making their own way toward the Light. Your second journey is the fun you have after enlightenment. It is, of course, not a journey, as there is nowhere to go. Your life now, as ever, is the result of the choices you make.

"What did you choose, Jay?"

Most of us left your world a long time ago. Some of us moved to different realities and different worlds and some went Home. Once we withdrew from your world it seems the love, magic and mystery gradually disappeared too. Sadly, men created religions and politico-economic systems to influence, control and enslave vast populations. Power and greed now dominate your planet.

"Yes, I remember you saying ..."

There are very few of us still on your planet. There are many of us who travel from the Light to assist different realities, including your world. I am one of those beings. We tread quietly and teach the eternal truths: loving-kindness, responsibility for fellow beings and responsibility for your world.

"Will the teachers be returning to our world soon?"

Yes, in time. Remember, every individual has the choice of how to live Now. You may choose to work as a political activist or social worker or as a doctor among the poor, but everyone has the ability to make a difference in their own way. Anyone can spread a little loving-kindness. Everyone has a voice. Why wait for the return of the teachers?

"If I choose to stay in this reality ..."

If you decide to stay in this reality as an enlightened being, you can work actively to help others, you can teach the truth, you can be a business manager, you can be a car mechanic ... whatever you prefer. Remember, it is not words that move others to the Light, nor what you do for a living ... it's the transmission of energy from the enlightened person.

"I am free to work and play as I choose ..."

Jay is staring out into the distance. *Sometimes words help too, Steve. Words are seeds that fall into the soil made fertile by enlightened energy. You could share your experiences ...*

"You mean ... like a write a book?"

Now there's an idea ...

"Seriously? I am not a writer. I have no idea how to write."

It's just words on paper. Life dancing on pages.

"Are you suggesting I write about my spiritual journey? And your mystical teachings?"

This world is in need of hope and truth. Every being wishes to discover its true nature and come Home. People are seeking a path to Awakening and your book will show the way. As more people reach enlightenment, the closer your entire planet moves to Awakening. Imagine your world ...

"If words are seeds ... then where is the enlightened energy? How will a book help people discover their true nature?"

Jay gets up and gives me a loving hug. He looks me gently in the eyes. *Do you know that a book written by an enlightened being will contain enlightened energy? Do you realise that people can move toward awakening from reading such a book?*

I frown and rub my eyebrow. "How can a book contain enlightened energy?"

Jay is beginning to shimmer. The light around him is pure white and becoming brighter. He puts his hand on his heart and those cobalt blue eyes lock onto mine.

Many people have heard of the Light, and some stand near the Light and preach to others about its bliss. Yet few have actually entered into the Light. Your book will reveal a path to Enlightenment and your enlightened energy will show the way Home.

Jay gives me a last loving smile and disappears. I lay outstretched on the soft grass and feel the warm sun drenching my body. Far above me a huge eagle is gliding across the perfect blue sky. I laugh freely. I am ready to begin the next journey.

About The Author

Stephen Shaw is an Enlightened Spiritual Teacher and Author. His books, consultations and seminars aim to raise world consciousness and contribute to global peace and spiritual awakening.

Stephen's first book **I Am** contains spiritual and mystical teachings from enlightened masters that point the way to love, peace, bliss, freedom and spiritual awakening.

Stephen's second book **Heart Song** takes you on a mystical adventure into creating your reality and manifesting your dreams, and reveals the secrets to attaining a fulfilled and joyful life.

Stephen's third book **Star Child** offers an exciting glimpse into the future on earth. The return of the gods and the advanced mystical teachings. And the ultimate battle of light versus darkness.

Stephen's fourth book **They Walk Among Us** is a love story spanning two realities. Explore the mystery of the angels. Discover the secrets of Love Whispering.

Stephen's fifth book **Reflections** offers mystical words for guidance, meditation and contemplation. Open the book anywhere and unwrap your daily inspiration.

For more information about Stephen's books, visit:
www.i-am-stephen-shaw.com